CHEMICAL DEPENDENCY
OPPOSING VIEWPOINTS®

OTHER BOOKS OF RELATED INTEREST

OPPOSING VIEWPOINTS SERIES

AIDS
America's Cities
America's Prisons
Child Abuse
Civil Liberties
Crime and Criminals
The Death Penalty
Drug Abuse
Gangs
The Homeless
Juvenile Crime
Mental Illness
Suicide
Violence
War on Drugs

CURRENT CONTROVERSIES SERIES

Alcoholism
Drug Trafficking
Smoking
Teen Addiction
Youth Violence

AT ISSUE SERIES

Legalizing Drugs
Smoking
The Spread of AIDS

CHEMICAL DEPENDENCY
OPPOSING VIEWPOINTS®

David L. Bender, *Publisher*
Bruno Leone, *Executive Editor*
Scott Barbour, *Managing Editor*
Brenda Stalcup, *Senior Editor*
Carol Wekesser, *Book Editor*

OPPOSING
VIEWPOINTS®
SERIES

Greenhaven Press, Inc., San Diego, California

Cover photo: Gazelle Technologies

Library of Congress Cataloging-in-Publication Data

Chemical dependency : opposing viewpoints / Carol Wekesser, book
    editor.
        p.   cm. — (Opposing viewpoints series)
    Includes bibliographical references and index.
    ISBN 1-56510-552-4 (lib. bdg. : alk. paper). —
ISBN 1-56510-551-6 (pbk. : alk. paper)
    1. Drug abuse—United States. 2. Alcoholism—United States.
3. Drug abuse—United States—Prevention. 4. Alcoholism—United
States—Prevention. I. Wekesser, Carol, 1963–   . II. Series.
HV5825.C44 1997
362.29'0973—dc21   96-48030
                                                                          CIP

Greenhaven Press, Inc., P.O. Box 289009
San Diego, CA 92198-9009

"CONGRESS SHALL MAKE NO LAW...ABRIDGING THE FREEDOM OF SPEECH, OR OF THE PRESS."

First Amendment to the U.S. Constitution

The basic foundation of our democracy is the First Amendment guarantee of freedom of expression. The Opposing Viewpoints Series is dedicated to the concept of this basic freedom and the idea that it is more important to practice it than to enshrine it.

CONTENTS

Why Consider Opposing Viewpoints?

"The only way in which a human being can make some approach to knowing the whole of a subject is by hearing what can be said about it by persons of every variety of opinion and studying all modes in which it can be looked at by every character of mind. No wise man ever acquired his wisdom in any mode but this."

John Stuart Mill

In our media-intensive culture it is not difficult to find differing opinions. Thousands of newspapers and magazines and dozens of radio and television talk shows resound with differing points of view. The difficulty lies in deciding which opinion to agree with and which "experts" seem the most credible. The more inundated we become with differing opinions and claims, the more essential it is to hone critical reading and thinking skills to evaluate these ideas. Opposing Viewpoints books address this problem directly by presenting stimulating debates that can be used to enhance and teach these skills. The varied opinions contained in each book examine many different aspects of a single issue. While examining these conveniently edited opposing views, readers can develop critical thinking skills such as the ability to compare and contrast authors' credibility, facts, argumentation styles, use of persuasive techniques, and other stylistic tools. In short, the Opposing Viewpoints Series is an ideal way to attain the higher-level thinking and reading skills so essential in a culture of diverse and contradictory opinions.

In addition to providing a tool for critical thinking, Opposing Viewpoints books challenge readers to question their own strongly held opinions and assumptions. Most people form their opinions on the basis of upbringing, peer pressure, and personal, cultural, or professional bias. By reading carefully balanced opposing views, readers must directly confront new ideas as well as the opinions of those with whom they disagree. This is not to simplistically argue that everyone who reads opposing views will—or should—change his or her opinion. Instead, the series enhances readers' understanding of their own views by encouraging confrontation with opposing ideas. Careful examination of others' views can lead to the readers' understanding of the logical inconsistencies in their own opinions, perspective on why they hold an opinion, and the consideration of the possibility that their opinion requires further evaluation.

EVALUATING OTHER OPINIONS

To ensure that this type of examination occurs, Opposing Viewpoints books present all types of opinions. Prominent spokespeople on different sides of each issue as well as well-known professionals from many disciplines challenge the reader. An additional goal of the series is to provide a forum for other, less known, or even unpopular viewpoints. The opinion of an ordinary person who has had to make the decision to cut off life support from a terminally ill relative, for example, may be just as valuable and provide just as much insight as a medical ethicist's professional opinion. The editors have two additional purposes in including these less known views. One, the editors encourage readers to respect others' opinions—even when not enhanced by professional credibility. It is only by reading or listening to and objectively evaluating others' ideas that one can determine whether they are worthy of consideration. Two, the inclusion of such viewpoints encourages the important critical thinking skill of objectively evaluating an author's credentials and bias. This evaluation will illuminate an author's reasons for taking a particular stance on an issue and will aid in readers' evaluation of the author's ideas.

As series editors of the Opposing Viewpoints Series, it is our hope that these books will give readers a deeper understanding of the issues debated and an appreciation of the complexity of even seemingly simple issues when good and honest people disagree. This awareness is particularly important in a democratic society such as ours in which people enter into public debate to determine the common good. Those with whom one disagrees should not be regarded as enemies but rather as people whose views deserve careful examination and may shed light on one's own.

Thomas Jefferson once said that "difference of opinion leads to inquiry, and inquiry to truth." Jefferson, a broadly educated man, argued that "if a nation expects to be ignorant and free . . . it expects what never was and never will be." As individuals and as a nation, it is imperative that we consider the opinions of others and examine them with skill and discernment. The Opposing Viewpoints Series is intended to help readers achieve this goal.

David L. Bender & Bruno Leone,
Series Editors

INTRODUCTION

"Of all the tyrannies which have usurped power over humanity, few have been able to enslave the mind and body as imperiously as . . . addiction."

Freda Adler, Sisters in Crime, 1975.

Chemical addictions—whether to alcohol, cocaine, heroin, or other substances—exact an enormous toll on addicted individuals, their families, and society as a whole. Alcoholism costs the United States an estimated $86 billion a year in health care costs and reduced productivity, while federal drug control programs cost about $15 billion annually. These figures do not include the amount that local and state agencies spend on drug programs, the amount all government agencies spend fighting alcoholism, and the costs of crime and lost productivity caused by drug abuse. These monetary figures also cannot measure the emotional and social price paid by addicts and their families.

Despite the high cost of addiction, helping addicts to stop using drugs or alcohol is often difficult. Many addicts never overcome their addiction, and those who do often require at least three courses of treatment to successfully combat drugs or alcohol. Most experts believe that in order to succeed, addicts *themselves* must want to be "clean and sober"; in other words, no treatments will be effective if the addict is not motivated from within to change.

Treatments for addiction vary, depending on the chemical involved, the individual addict's history, and the available resources. The most common form of treatment for alcoholism and drug addiction involves detoxification followed by education, counseling, and participation in a twelve-step program such as Alcoholics Anonymous. Depending on the individual, this process can involve various combinations of outpatient and inpatient hospitalization. Heroin addiction is often treated with methadone, a drug that ameliorates the withdrawal symptoms produced by the cessation of heroin use. Numerous alternative treatments—including acupuncture, meditation, and aversion therapy—are also utilized in the battle to end addiction.

In the past few years, some researchers have experimented with rewarding addicts with food, money, or clothing if the addict commits to and/or completes a course of treatment. For example, Stephen T. Higgins, professor of psychiatry at the University of Vermont, oversees a treatment program that uses store vouchers as rewards for addicts who continue treatment for two months. In a study sponsored by the National Institute on Drug Abuse, Higgins found that 90 percent of addicts in a voucher-incentive group remained drug-free after twelve weeks, compared to 65 percent in a non-voucher group. After twenty-four weeks, the success rates were 75 percent and 40 percent, respectively. Vouchers provide "a big incentive to sustain long periods of abstinence," states Kenneth Silverman, assistant professor of psychiatry at Johns Hopkins University School of Medicine.

Other substance abuse experts, however, question the usefulness of vouchers. They contend that while vouchers may tempt people to remain sober for a short period of time, they are ineffective at helping people become permanently clean. "Rewards, like punishment, can never buy anything but temporary compliance," argues Alfie Kohn, author of the book *Punished by Rewards*. Even Silverman acknowledges that voucher systems do little to prevent relapse among addicts.

While some people debate the effectiveness of vouchers and similar programs, others question the entire concept of rewarding addicts for staying clean. Some commentators insist that addicts should be punished rather than paid. As former drug czar William Bennett states, "Those who use, sell and traffic in drugs must be confronted, and they must suffer consequences. By 'consequences,' I mean . . . the seizure of assets, stiffer prison sentences, revocation of bail rights, and the death penalty for drug kingpins."

Whether substance abusers should be rewarded for staying clean or punished for breaking the law is just one of the issues debated in *Chemical Dependency: Opposing Viewpoints*. This anthology explores the nature of addiction and its causes and cures in the following chapters: How Great a Problem Is Chemical Dependency? What Causes Chemical Dependency? What Treatments Are Effective for Chemical Dependency? Should Drug Laws Be Reformed? Chemical dependency is a serious, devastating problem—both for the addict and for society in general. By reading and examining a wide array of opinions concerning addiction to chemicals, it is hoped the reader will gain a better understanding of why this problem is so intractable and why it generates so much discussion.

CHAPTER 1

HOW GREAT A PROBLEM IS CHEMICAL DEPENDENCY?

CHAPTER PREFACE

People have used intoxicating substances since they first discovered that eating or smoking certain plants was relaxing or stimulating. Gradually, the use of such plants took on more meaning and importance in human civilization. The use of wine, beer, and drugs such as opium and marijuana became ritualistic in some cultures. For example, peyote, a nonaddictive hallucinogenic drug derived from cactus, is eaten as a sacramental food by the Navajos and other Native American tribes. Alcohol is often used symbolically by Christians and Jews. People also use intoxicating substances at formal celebrations such as weddings and at informal gatherings such as weekend parties.

Using alcohol and drugs for rituals or celebrations is accepted in many societies. But *abusing* intoxicating substances is often not tolerated because of the physical, psychological, and social consequences for the intoxicated person and others. Accidents caused by drunk drivers, child abuse by addicted parents, and poor job performance by addicted employees are just a few of the negative consequences of addiction.

Unfortunately, it is not always easy to define the difference between *using* and *abusing* intoxicating substances. What substance is being used, how addictive it is, how much of it is being used, and who is using it are some of the questions people ask as they try to determine if a substance is harmful. For example, most people agree that because it is extremely addictive, heroin is dangerous. However, some disagreement exists concerning the risk of overdose from heroin. Hundreds of deaths are attributed to heroin overdose each year. But according to Stanton Peele, the author of several books on addiction, many of these deaths actually result from combining heroin with other drugs such as alcohol and cocaine. Peele argues that the risk of overdose from heroin alone is much lower than is commonly believed.

The contributors to the following chapter discuss the potential harm heroin, alcohol, and marijuana pose to individuals and society. They explain why they believe these substances are harmful or benign, and they discuss social and governmental policies to either restrict or encourage the use of these substances.

"The bad news is heroin
is back."

HEROIN USE IS A SERIOUS PROBLEM

John Leland

In the following viewpoint, John Leland suggests that heroin use, which has increased in recent years, could be the next major drug problem in the United States. New users have been attracted to heroin because of its increased purity and low price, Leland writes. While most new users begin by snorting the substance, according to Leland, many progress to injecting it, placing them at risk of HIV infection and overdose. Leland is a senior writer for *Newsweek* magazine.

As you read, consider the following questions:

1. How much has heroin use increased since the 1980s, according to the author?
2. Why is it difficult to determine the number of affluent heroin users, according to Leland?
3. How many people die of heroin overdoses annually, according to Leland?

Jane Howland likes to try an experiment when she talks to kids about drugs. Howland is a middle-school guidance counselor in Greenwich, Connecticut, one of the wealthiest suburbs in America. The kids are maybe 10 or 11. "I ask them who knows what it means to be a high-risk-taker," she says. Every hand goes up. Then she asks those who consider themselves high-risk-takers to go to one part of the room, low- and middle-riskers to another. Invariably, every boy goes to the high-risk group. "They push each other out of the way to get there first. It's cool." These are just pre-teens; to them risk means shoplifting, vandalism, marijuana, maybe inhalants. But many of her fifth graders are in the thrall of Kurt Cobain; they think he was "really cool," she says. Howland worries that, by the eighth and ninth grades, the biggest risk-takers might want to follow Cobain's path into heroin.

Heroin Use Is on the Rise

After a decade in low relief, heroin is now scaring the heck out of people like Howland, in cities and suburbs nationwide. "The bad news," says Gen. Barry McCaffrey, the new drug czar, "is heroin is back." Schools that used to discuss heroin in the late high-school years now teach it in the eighth grade. The Partnership for a Drug-Free America, best known for its "This is your brain on drugs" campaign of the '80s, now worries that heroin will be the drug of the '90s. . . . In 1996 the organization rolled out the most expensive publicity campaign ever to target heroin. Spurred by images of junkie celebs, and anecdotes about middle-class heroin use, the press has touted a new epidemic since 1989. Now, says Yale medical historian David Musto, "this is the nearest we've come."

How near are we? The answers are not so clear. There are an estimated 500,000 to 750,000 heroin addicts in this country, a figure that has held steady for decades. But since 1991, heroin use has been on the rise. Since heroin is illegal, no one knows just how many people use it. But by rough government estimates, U.S. heroin consumption has doubled since the mid-'80s, to about 10 to 15 metric tons per year. In 1996, 2.3 percent of eighth graders said they had tried heroin, nearly double the rate of 1991. (Note: eighth graders always show higher rates than high-schoolers, because heroin users tend to drop out of school.) "Obviously this is not a runaway epidemic among teens," says Lloyd Johnston of the University of Michigan, who monitors adolescent drug use. "But it should give rise to some caution."

Most heroin users today are still old-timers, battered by decades of addiction, arrest and rehab. As crack use has stabilized, many crack smokers have also turned to heroin to ease their cocaine jitters. Dealers, increasingly, are "double breasting," or selling both—bringing crack's widespread availability to heroin. But in many cities, a new class of user is emerging. Drug ethnographers Ansley Hamid and Ric Curtis of John Jay College of Criminal Justice note that as residents of black and Latino communities turned away from heroin in the early '90s, white people started to show up, "infatuated with it," says Curtis. The numbers of new, more affluent users are especially elusive. Because they have resources, they tend not to show up in jail or public treatment centers. "Heroin may be flying *above* the radar," says Mark A.R. Kleiman, a drug-policy analyst at UCLA [University of California-Los Angeles].

WHY HEROIN AND WHY NOW?

If the U.S. auto industry cut the price of its sedans by half and redesigned them to go 180 mph, no one would wonder why sales hit the roof. Since 1991 the heroin industry—a $7 billion-plus retail market in the United States—has wrought a similar revolution, offering a more powerful, cheaper and safer product. In the '80s average $10 bags ran about 2 to 8 percent pure; by 1994 average purity in New York hit 63 percent—pure enough to snort or smoke, without the risk of getting AIDS from dirty needles. This made the drug seem less deadly, more approachable. At the same time, the price has fallen to a historic low. The street price of a milligram in New York fell from $1.81 in 1988 to just 37 cents in 1994. Globally, heroin production doubled between 1986 and 1996, flooding the United States from Burma, Afghanistan, Laos, Pakistan, Colombia and Mexico—and ensuring a competitive market with low prices and high purity. As a White House report conceded, "We have yet to substantially influence either the availability or the purity of cocaine and heroin within the United States."

Heroin's rise is also historically predictable. Since 1885 cocaine and opiate waves have succeeded one another, each relieving the chronic maladies of the last. Cocaine epidemics tend to be fast and short, accelerated by binge use. "You can't take cocaine for long periods of time," says Herbert Kleber of the Center on Addiction and Substance Abuse at Columbia University. "It burns you out. People need a sedative to mellow out: sometimes alcohol, sometimes heroin." Heroin booms, by contrast, move slowly. Users take an average of three to 10 years to progress from regular use to treatment or arrest. The heroin horror stories circulating now suggest a rise in use four or five years ago, and may signal the start of a decline. As Kleber notes, "All drug cycles carry the seed of their own destruction."

Eighth Graders Who Have Used Drugs in Their Lifetime (in Percent)			
	1991	1995	percent change
Crack	1.3	2.7	**+108**
Heroin	1.2	2.3	**+92**
Marijuana	10.2	19.9	**+95**
Cocaine	2.3	4.2	**+83**
Hallucinogens	3.2	5.2	**+63**
Stimulants	10.5	13.1	**+25**
Tranquilizers	3.8	4.5	**+18**
Cigarettes	44.0	46.4	**+5**
Been drunk	26.7	25.3	**−5**

Source: University of Michigan, Monitoring the Future Study.

New users typically begin by snorting. But many progress to the more efficient method of injecting. According to General McCaffrey, about 50 percent of users seeking treatment in 1995 used needles; in 1996, the figure had grown to 75 percent. This is doubly dangerous. Injection-drug users now have the highest rates of new HIV infection, nearly twice that of gay men. And wild fluctuations in street purity raise the risk of overdose. Between 3,000 and 4,000 users die of heroin overdoses annually—many using the heroin in lethal combination with alcohol or other drugs. The expanding drug market and the criminal-justice system unwittingly conspire to push this figure higher. As police arrest drug consumers by the thousands, as part of the war on drugs, users are likely to come out of jail with reduced tolerance—and a lower threshold for overdose. Also, says John Jay College's Curtis, some new dealers don't have experience with the substance. He mentions one experienced Brooklyn dealer known as Half, for the way he cuts the dope. "The new guys turn to him to show them how it's done." Others, though, "use too much adulterant, or too little," giving people unpredictably strong doses. "I attribute deaths to that instability."

It is too soon to say how high the current heroin wave will rise, or how long it will last. Musto of Yale contends that it "won't be as alarming as the last [in the '70s], because we're much better informed about drugs now. The number of people the 'chic' aspect applies to is very small." But many professionals believe we can't wait around to find out. Already there are too few treatment slots for the addicts on the streets, a woeful short- age of treatment beds in prisons—and no money for more. Wayne Wiebel, an epidemiologist at the University of Illinois at Chicago, offers a chilling scenario. We are unprepared, he says, especially to help the young users just getting hooked. "There are only two pots of money," says Wiebel. "One is for preven- tion, mostly through schools; and the other is treatment for ca- sualties that have already been fully impacted by the problem. There's virtually nothing in the middle for early intervention." Wiebel has been studying drug trends for more than 15 years. From where he stands, the new wave of heroin use, and our re- action to it, looks horrifyingly familiar. It's going to "unfold like the crack epidemic," he says, "and we're not going to do a hell of a lot about it."

"*A ... search ... has failed to turn up a single scientific paper reporting that heroin overdose ... is in fact a cause of death among American heroin addicts.*"

THE PROBLEM OF HEROIN USE IS EXAGGERATED

Stanton Peele

Stanton Peele is a psychologist and health care researcher and the author of several books on addiction, including *The Truth About Addiction and Recovery: The Life Process for Outgrowing Destructive Habits*. In the following viewpoint, Peele criticizes the media for exaggerating the extent of America's heroin problem. Peele does not deny that heroin can be a dangerous drug, but he insists that true heroin overdoses are rare and that most of the problems attributed to heroin are caused by other substances used in combination with heroin.

As you read, consider the following questions:

1. What evidence does the author give to support his argument that it is difficult to overdose on heroin?
2. What four assumptions prevent the mainstream press from accurately reporting on drugs, in Peele's opinion?

Stanton Peele, "Hype Overdose," *National Review*, November 7, 1994. Copyright ©1994 by National Review, Inc., 150 E. 35th St., New York, NY 10016. Reprinted by permission.

On August 31, 1994, a headline on the front page of the *New York Times* reported: "13 Heroin Deaths Spark Wide Police Investigation." The article began: "They call it China Cat, an exotic name for a blend of heroin so pure it promised a perfect high, but instead killed thirteen people in five days." In less time than that, the story started to unravel.

On September 2, a brief article in the *Times'* B section announced: "Officials Lower Number of Deaths Related to Concentrated Heroin." By this time, published reports had attributed fourteen deaths to China Cat. But now the *Times* reported that "authorities yesterday lowered from fourteen to eight the number of deaths in the last week that the police believe are related to highly concentrated heroin." The medical examiner had discovered that "two of the fourteen men originally suspected of having died from taking the powerful heroin had actually died of natural causes. Four others died of overdoses of cocaine. . . . Of the eight whose deaths apparently did involve heroin, seven also had traces of cocaine in their system."

No Apology

Thus, deaths that had been attributed to heroin overdose were now only "suspected" overdose deaths. Yet the *Times* felt no need to retract or apologize for its original report, simply attributing the overestimate to "authorities." Furthermore, six of the fourteen people (42 per cent) reported to have died of heroin overdoses had in fact not taken any heroin (two hadn't taken any drugs at all), while 92 per cent of the men who had died after taking drugs had taken cocaine, compared with 67 per cent who had taken heroin.

Given these facts, you might wonder how the "authorities" and the *Times* decided that so many men had died of China Cat. According to the second article, "the police said they found packets of China Cat, the street name of a powerful heroin blend, and a syringe" beside the body of *one* dead man. "They had no similar evidence connecting the China Cat brand to the other victims, but . . . they considered it probable that a purer blend of heroin was involved" (even with those who, it turned out, had taken no heroin).

The cavalier attitude with which America's leading newspaper reported speculation and misinformation as fact illustrates the reluctance of the mainstream press to question negative statements about drugs, no matter how ill founded. When such statements turn out to be wrong, readers are not likely to see an apology or even an explicit correction. For many news outlets, reporting bad things about illegal substances is part of a moral mission aimed at discouraging drug use, a mission that makes truth secondary.

So it's not surprising that the *Times* continued to pursue the overdose story even after it had become clear that the scare had little basis in fact. A front-page article on September 4 reported: "At first, the police suspected that the men . . . had all died after using an extremely potent blend of heroin called China Cat. . . . Now the police and the New York City Medical Examiner, Dr. Charles Hirsch, say the men may have been victims of that brand or some similar, equally powerful blends of heroin. . . . But as one police officer put it: 'They're all still dead.' In the end, drug experts said, the brand name probably has little significance."

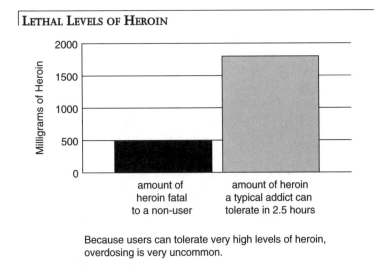

LETHAL LEVELS OF HEROIN

Because users can tolerate very high levels of heroin, overdosing is very uncommon.

Source: Stanton Peele, *National Review*, November 7, 1994.

Maybe, but China Cat was central to the original article. Furthermore, six of the men had not taken heroin at all. And even for the ones who had, there was no evidence of *overdose*. Given the results from the blood tests, it is more plausible that the men died from a mix of drugs, including cocaine, alcohol, and perhaps other substances.

GROUNDS FOR SKEPTICISM

Indeed, researchers who have studied the issue closely are skeptical about reports of heroin "overdoses" in general. In the 1972 book *Licit and Illicit Drugs*, Edward M. Brecher summarized the evidence that led him to conclude that all or nearly all such deaths are in fact due to other causes. Based on experiments with animals, toxicologists estimate that it would take at least 500 milligrams of heroin to kill an adult human being who is not addicted to the drug; and studies of addicts find that they can typically tolerate as much as 1,800 milligrams over a two-and-a-half-hour period. In research conducted at Philadelphia's Jefferson Medical Center in the 1920s, addicts who were injected with up to nine times their ordinary daily dose suffered no ill effects.

The historical record also offers grounds for skepticism about heroin "overdoses." In New York City, before 1943, deaths among heroin addicts were rarely described as overdoses. Between 1943 and 1970, the percentage of addict deaths attributed to overdose climbed to about 80 per cent. Yet heroin purity was falling steadily during this period. In the 1920s addicts reported daily doses forty times as concentrated as the typical New York City daily dose in the 1970s.

Big-city coroners, Brecher noted, tend to record as overdose deaths any cases involving addicts (or, as in the *Times* story, men who look like addicts) where there is no other obvious cause of death. "A conscientious search of the United States medical literature throughout recent decades," he wrote, "has failed to turn up a single scientific paper reporting that heroin overdose, as established by . . . reasonable methods of determining overdose, is in fact a cause of death among American heroin addicts."

Brecher reviewed research by two prominent New York City medical examiners, Drs. Milton Helpern and Michael Baden, who examined New York City addict deaths in the 1960s. Helpern and Baden reported that the heroin found near the dead addicts was not unusually pure and that their body tissues did not show especially high concentrations of the drug. Although the addicts typically shot up in groups, only one addict at a time died. Furthermore, the dead addicts were experienced rather than novice users and therefore should have built up tolerance to large doses of heroin.

INTERACTION

It is instructive to bear Brecher's points in mind while reading the articles in the *Times*. The third and most detailed article described the supposed heroin-overdose death of Gregory Ancona, the only case in which an eyewitness account was available. When Ancona and a date returned from a club to his apartment, he "was already staggering from the effects of cocaine and alcohol." While his date injected her heroin, Ancona snorted his.

"Soon after, he nodded off and never woke up." The woman, meanwhile, "suffered no more than the usual effects of heroin."

From this account, it seems unlikely that Ancona died of an overdose. To begin with, men generally weigh more than women and show milder reactions to a given drug. Furthermore, he snorted the heroin, while his date injected it, getting more of the drug into her bloodstream more quickly. The probable cause of Ancona's death is the interaction of drug effects, particularly those of alcohol and heroin, which research suggests can be lethal.

UNINTENDED CONSEQUENCES

In this connection, careless reporting about heroin "overdoses" can have a perverse effect. If an addict believed that the real hazard was dosage, he might not recognize the dangers of combining drugs. In Ancona's case, he might have thought he was protecting himself from a heroin overdose by snorting the drug rather than injecting it. Moreover, Drs. Helpern and Baden concluded that impurities in heroin (particularly quinine) are more likely than the drug itself to be the culprit in addict deaths. If so, the most adulterated (impure) doses of heroin may be the most dangerous—exactly the opposite of the message communicated by the *Times*.

Like most of the mainstream press, the *Times* is blind to such unintended consequences, because of its own assumptions:

1. *Drugs are so bad that any negative claim about them is justified.* The *Times* will not be called to task for inaccuracy in reporting about drugs, as it might if it reported with similar credulity about crime or politics.

2. *Heroin is the worst drug.* On the face of it, the *Times* could have made a better case for the toxicity of cocaine based on the fourteen cited deaths, yet it chose to focus on heroin.

3. *Blaming drug deaths on overdose is important for propaganda purposes.* The press assumes that reports about purer heroin will deter drug use.

4. *Heroin use and addiction have shifted to the middle class.* The *Times* stressed that several of the dead men were middle-class.

These notions are both dubious and counterproductive. But you won't read about that in the *New York Times*.

| "We have yet to come to terms with
the vast damage that alcohol can do."

ALCOHOL ABUSE IS A SERIOUS PROBLEM

Anna Quindlen

In the following viewpoint, Anna Quindlen argues that while most Americans are quick to acknowledge the harms of illicit drugs and tobacco, they are less willing to admit the many ways alcohol destroys lives and harms society. Quindlen contends that alcohol is especially a problem among college-age Americans: Alcohol is involved in 90 percent of the rapes and two-thirds of the suicides on college campuses. The author concludes that Americans must face their problems with alcohol and educate young people about its dangers. Quindlen is an author and a former columnist for the *New York Times*.

As you read, consider the following questions:
1. How might children be confused by adults' messages concerning alcohol, in Quindlen's opinion?
2. What comparisons does the author make between the harms of alcohol and the harms of illegal drugs to society?
3. Why do so many young people drink, according to Quindlen?

Anna Quindlen, "The Legal Drug," *New York Times*, June 11, 1994. Copyright ©1994 by The New York Times Company, Inc. Reprinted by permission.

For some it is a beverage, for some a habit, for some an addiction.

And those differences, perhaps more than anything else, explain why we have yet to come to terms with the vast damage that alcohol can do, with those it kills, those it harms, those who can't get loose from its sharp fishhook.

While even young children know that cocaine and heroin are nothing but trouble, while even young children know that cigarettes cause cancer, what they know and learn and believe about booze and beer and wine is different because it is the drug their parents keep in the refrigerator and use themselves. And that can be confusing.

The Center on Addiction and Substance Abuse at Columbia University has quantified some of the results of that confusion. A commission report shows that "binge drinking is the number one substance abuse problem in American college life," far outweighing the use of drugs. The widespread use of alcohol at nearly every American school affects everything from the prevalence of venereal disease to the failure rate.

Ninety percent of all reported campus rapes occur when either the victim or the assailant has been drinking. At least one in five college students abandons safe sex practices when drunk that they'd use when sober. Two-thirds of college suicide victims were legally intoxicated at the time of death. Estimates of alcoholism range from 10 to 15 percent of the college population.

What's wrong with this picture? These statistics would normally be the stuff of vocal lobbies, calls for action and regulation. Instead alcohol manufacturers openly court the college market, advertising in campus newspapers despite the fact that many of the readers are too young to drink legally. In a 1991 report on alcohol promotion on campus, one marketing executive was quoted on the importance of developing brand loyalty in a student. "If he turns out to be a big drinker, the beer company has bought itself an annuity," the executive said.

"When parents visit, their concern is drugs," said one college administrator. "They're surprised if we want to talk about drinking. A few are even annoyed."

The demonization of drugs allows delusion about alcohol to flourish. There are 18.5 million people with alcohol problems and only 5 million drug addicts. More people who commit crimes are drunk than high. Illicit drug use on campus has decreased 60 percent in the last decade. Beer is the dope of the quad.

Colleges and universities are cautious in confronting alcohol use on campus; if they accept responsibility for policing it, administrators are concerned they will be held legally responsible for its effects. And for many parents, the legality of alcohol is a convenient excuse not to delve too deeply into the issues it raises for their kids, issues not only about drinking but about self-image. Research being done at Mississippi State University showed that many students drank to escape from anger and loneliness, to feel accepted and at ease.

BINGE DRINKERS

A new survey of four-year college student alcohol and other drug use conducted by the Harvard School of Public Health confirmed that the United States continues to have a major substance use problem on its college campuses. . . .

Many students are still drinking a great deal. This is true even among students under the minimum drinking age. Especially worrisome is the percentage of college students who are heavy or problem drinkers.

William DeJong and Stacia Langenbahn, *Setting and Improving Policies for Reducing Alcohol and Other Drug Problems on Campus: A Guide for School Administrators*, 1996.

College authorities and parents both have to find some way to communicate that using alcohol to anesthetize doubt and insecurity can become a lifelong habit as fast as you can say A.A. And that way lies disaster, disappointment, even death. The other day Betty Ford came with her daughter, Susan, to a symposium at the Center on Addiction and Substance Abuse so both could talk about how her family had to force her into treatment. "I suddenly found myself making excuses so that I wouldn't have to spend too much time over at the house," Susan said of the time when the former First Lady was addicted to booze and pills.

Cynthia Gorney, in an exquisite essay in the *Washington Post*, wrote of her mother: ". . . she was a woman of curiosity and learning and great intelligence. She died in March, of cirrhosis of the liver, which is also what kills the men under blankets by the sewer grates."

But kids won't even begin to understand that until everyone starts to treat alcohol like what it is: a legal drug. That can be confusing too, since there are many who can drink with no ill effect and never come close to addiction. But just because many of us are safe drivers doesn't mean we don't acknowledge the existence of car accidents. And in the lives of many young adults, alcohol is an accident waiting to happen.

| "Drinking of alcoholic beverages can be good for you."

ALCOHOL CAN BE BENEFICIAL

Dwight Heath

Dwight Heath is a member of the advisory board of the American Council on Science and Health, a New York–based research organization that focuses on public health issues. In the following viewpoint, Heath discusses research showing that moderate drinking is better for one's health than abstaining from alcohol. He contends that the government has for too long emphasized the risk of excessive drinking while downplaying the benefits of moderate drinking.

As you read, consider the following questions:

1. What are some of the health benefits of alcohol cited by Heath?
2. Why does the author discourage people from thinking of alcohol as health food?
3. What are some reasons *not* to drink, in Heath's opinion?

The U.S. government has made an about-face: It now admits that moderate drinking of alcoholic beverages can be good for you—conceding what the majority of people around the world have believed for centuries and what scientific research repeatedly has confirmed.

A new revision of the "Dietary Guidelines for Americans"—issued by the Departments of Agriculture and Health and Human Services—reverses an earlier warning that "drinking has no net health benefit" and admits that "there is accumulating evidence that moderate drinking may lower the risk of heart disease."

The "Dietary Guidelines" booklet may never be a best-seller, but it does get attention: from medical personnel and educators who are concerned with health and nutrition, from corporations that use it for advertising, from consumers and from those who manage various federal food programs.

For many years, our bureaucrats have been eager enough to chronicle—in excruciating detail—the risks of excessive drinking. The campaign was conducted with such zeal one agency was censured by the General Accounting Office for illegally lobbying against alcohol.

EVIDENCE IN SUPPORT OF ALCOHOL

By contrast, the bureaucrats ignored—or, worse yet, denied—the rapidly mounting and well-documented benefits of moderate drinking. Most important among these is protection against coronary heart disease, the major cause of death among adults in most industrial nations.

Several studies on large and diverse populations from around the world agree that both heavy drinkers and those who drink no alcohol at all have higher rates of death and illness from heart disease than do light or moderate drinkers. The dietary guidelines define "moderate drinking" as "no more than one drink a day for women and no more than two drinks a day for men." Several other countries have more liberal definitions.

Protection against coronary heart disease derives from a number of effects that alcohol has. Alcohol diminishes low-density lipoproteins (LDL), the harmful form of cholesterol; increases high-density lipoproteins (HDL), the protective cholesterol; decreases formation of blood clots in the arteries; increases coronary blood-flow; and enhances estrogen levels.

Other possible benefits, now being investigated, include lower rates of non-insulin-dependent (adult-onset) diabetes, rheumatoid arthritis and breast cancer, greater bone density, muscle strength, coordination, agility and balance and less depression.

It is important to keep in mind that most of the research on the benefits of moderate drinking has to do with large groups and cannot predict how moderate drinking will affect an individual. For that reason, scientists are not about to suggest that beer, wine or spirits should be viewed as health food, or even as suitable for everyone. There are some people who, for whatever reason, do not wish to drink; and that is probably their best choice. There are others who find it difficult to limit their drinking to a moderate level; they, too, should avoid the risk.

REASONS NOT TO DRINK

Young people, especially, should think hard about their reasons for drinking. There are those who expect alcohol to make them debonair; who want to demonstrate their maturity; who expect alcohol to enhance their sexuality; who want to forget their troubles; or who simply want to become so drunk that they no longer can be held responsible for their actions. Those people, young and old alike, are not only usually disappointed but often actually harmed by drinking.

By contrast, many people enjoy a small amount of alcohol as an enhancer of food, as a demonstration of hospitality or sociability; as a symbolic way to set off leisure hours from the workday; as part of a religious ceremony; or simply as a tasty, inexpensive and effective relaxant.

AS MUCH PLEASURE AS PAIN

If alcohol is indeed, as we are often told, "America's number-one drug problem," it is also probably America's number-one scapegoat for societal ills—ills whose real causes don't come conveniently packaged in bottle form.

And I think that, insofar as it is possible to measure such things, alcohol probably brings as much pleasure to the world as it brings pain. Plenty of people speak out against the pain. I think somebody ought to speak up for the pleasure.

Colman Andrews, *Los Angeles Times Magazine*, January 2, 1994.

Those people should not be frightened by the misinformation about the risks of moderate drinking. For the great majority of people those risks are few, and they are far outweighed by the benefit.

Isn't it nice at last to have authoritative support for that popular view?

| "Marijuana is
| 'dangerous stuff.'"

MARIJUANA IS HARMFUL

Michael Quintanilla

In the following viewpoint, Michael Quintanilla writes that society has failed to inform young people that marijuana is a dangerous drug. Quoting the views of several teenagers who describe their use of marijuana, the author notes that young people demonstrate a casual attitude toward drug use because they are unaware of the dangers involved. Because they mistakenly believe that drugs are relatively harmless, Quintanilla reports, an increasing number of teenagers are using marijuana and other drugs. Quintanilla is a staff writer for the *Los Angeles Times* newspaper.

As you read, consider the following questions:

1. Why do many teenagers use marijuana, according to the author?
2. Why has marijuana use among teenagers increased, according to Quintanilla?
3. Why do some teenagers refuse to use marijuana, according to the author?

Every Monday morning at Santa Monica High School [in Los Angeles, California], 15-year-old Becky chats up her friends about the weekend. Repeatedly, the conversation turns to the same topic: smoking-out at a raze party, getting lifted on blunts and chronic.

Translation: getting high on marijuana at a friend's house.

"Marijuana is the drug to do. It's cheap. It's easy to get. It's everywhere," says the freshman, whose name has been changed along with those of other teenagers in this viewpoint. "People smoke-out in the restrooms, during lunch. They ditch to smoke."

Across Los Angeles, some students are taking a fast, drug-laden trip fueled by an attitude that it's cool to smoke marijuana, not viewing the drug as addictive, harmful or a great risk, even though researchers warn that it is 20 times more potent today than in the 1960s and '70s.

ILLICIT DRUGS ON THE RISE

This attitude is in line with the findings of a University of Michigan study announced in 1994 that illicit drug use—with marijuana heading the list—among American teen-agers has increased, reversing a trend of generally declining use that began in the late '70s and early '80s.

Teen-agers who use pot say they are merely experimenting or smoking to fit in or to cope with the stress of problems at home and school. Most say they smoke marijuana—which currently also goes by names like "bud," "endo," "lovelies," "primos" and "frios"—when they're bored at school and simply because it's fun to do at parties.

At HPs (home parties) and DPs (ditching parties), teen-agers mix marijuana—ranging in price from $5 for a joint to $40 and more for a half-filled sandwich bag of the stuff—with crushed rock cocaine for a stronger high. They dip joints in solvents and insecticides and lace them with PCP, a powerful psychedelic drug that can cause mental or emotional disorders or death. Also popular are $5 LSD tabs—paper the size of a contact lens that has been blotted with a drop of the hallucinogen, which students suck on or place under an eyelid for a faster rush.

Felipe, a 10th-grader at a Los Angeles high school, says he has smoked marijuana daily for the past two years. "I am probably addicted to marijuana. I got plants at my home. I've gone to school crazy high. I get high 'cause my friends do it. It's fun, I guess."

The survey of 50,000 junior and high school students, conducted for the National Institute on Drug Abuse, found that marijuana and LSD, along with inhalants and stimulants, were being used by more teen-agers.

The study, widely regarded as one of the government's chief benchmarks for measuring progress in the drug war, found that cocaine use held steady at low levels, alcohol use generally declined, but cigarette use was on the rise.

According to the survey, the percentage of high school seniors who reported using an illicit drug at least once in their lives increased from 40.7% in 1992 to 42.9% in 1993, but still remained below the peak of 65.6% reported in a comparable study in 1981.

The survey also found that the proportion of eighth-graders using marijuana increased three percentage points between 1992 and 1993, to 9.2%. Among 10th-graders, the share using marijuana went from 15.2% in 1992 to 19.2% in 1993. The percentage of 12th-graders smoking the drug increased from 21.9% to 26% between 1992 and 1993, researchers reported.

GROWING COMPLACENCY

Researchers, parents, educators, law enforcement officials and drug treatment experts agree that the findings are troublesome. Most officials attribute the results to a growing complacency about the problems of drug abuse, peer pressure, a lack of attention to the issue by both government and the media, and too much freedom allowed by parents, especially those who came of age during an era when drug use was widely glamorized.

Ruth Rich, director of substance abuse programs for the Los Angeles Unified School District, confirmed that more students are seeking and being referred to support groups for the use of marijuana and LSD. "The reason is they're getting a lot of propaganda that using drugs is OK," she says, citing U.S. Surgeon General Joycelyn Elders and other public officials who have advocated legalization, or the study of it.

The increase is slight, however, and Los Angeles school district rates, which tend to mirror those nationally, have not returned to their 1978 peak, when 65% of high school students said they had tried an illegal substance at least once.

Michael Moran, a sergeant with the Los Angeles Police Department's DARE (Drug Abuse Resistance Education) program, says some of the biggest obstacles officers face are peer pressure and parental denial that "their little darling could be doing something wrong."

Moreover, he says, "We used to tell children, 'If you use drugs, bad things will happen to you.' It's not true. A lot of casual users go on for years and function in what we think is a normal life. Until they are no longer here, we are going to have a large number of people buying drugs and they will have a major impact on our youth."

THE SOCIAL THING TO DO

Despite official concern, the kids who are using pot say it is a pervasive and harmless pastime.

"Marijuana is not like crack. That messes you up bad," says Lorenzo, who has smoked marijuana for two years.

Lorenzo, a Los Angeles high school student, says he has managed to keep his secret from his parents. Ironically, his father is an alcohol and drug abuse counselor.

"If my dad knew, he'd probably throw me in rehab," he says. "My parents never told me about drugs, so I had to experiment with them myself. But when you experiment too much, you like it and then you get hooked."

He says he gets high because it's the social thing to do. Marijuana, he says, expands his imagination, relaxes him and helps him cope with problems at home. He realizes that smoking pot has had an adverse effect on him; his grade-point average has gone from a high C to a low D and he no longer plays interscholastic sports because he has become lethargic. Now he ditches classes to smoke and is out every weeknight, sometimes just kicking back with his friends or out clubbing. That usually includes getting high because "I can't have fun without bud [marijuana]."

THE EFFECTS OF MARIJUANA

There are many disturbing questions about marijuana's effect on the vital systems of the body, on the brain and mind, on immunity and resistance, and on sex and reproduction. . . . Recent research on the behavioral aspects of the drug suggests that it severely affects the social perceptions of heavy users. . . . The research subjects used marijuana to avoid dealing with their difficulties, and the avoidance inevitably made their problems worse —on the job, at home, and in family and sexual relationships.

James A. Inciardi and Duane C. McBride, *The Drug Legalization Debate*, 1991.

Julia, a 17-year-old senior at Ramona Opportunity School, says that since age 12, she has experimented with "everything except for heroin." At 14, she was selling rock cocaine to her friends.

"Lately, I've been smoking primos—weed mixed with rock

cocaine," she says, sitting at a picnic table. "I want some type of enjoyment. I kick it with my friends" at house parties, where she can select from a wide choice of drugs to use and buy. "We just walk into the house and ask them for a dime [$10] bag." If she buys from a friend, a dime bag usually goes for $2 or $3.

"Everybody is so used to marijuana in their system that they don't even get buzzed off of it no more. They just don't think it's dangerous," she says, adding that her friends are mixing marijuana with other drugs to sustain their highs.

"Yesterday, a girl was smoked out on a frio [marijuana laced with PCP]. Her eyes were drooping. The teachers sense it. They don't even say nothing. What can they do? Right now my friends are into smoking dust, marijuana with chemicals in it. It's a weird drug. One time my friend smoked it and he started to pretend he was a bird."

Julia says adults have told her and her friends that drugs are bad, but the attitude among her classmates is that "nobody cares to hear 'Just Say No.' Drugs are just part of society."

THOSE WHO DON'T SMOKE

Although the findings from the University of Michigan's study are disturbing, researchers point out that the numbers still are below the levels of the 1970s. They also report that the 42% of high school seniors who said they had used an illicit drug at least once in their lives is still a minority. And many kids say they have been influenced by warnings from parents and experts and have chosen to stay away from drugs.

Andrew, 16, a 10th-grader at George Washington Preparatory High School, tried marijuana once, didn't like it and vows never to do it again.

"I wanted to get high cause I had problems at home. Bud doesn't make you do bad things, it makes you lazy and later you fall asleep. I don't think it's a major big drug like crack, but I also know that it's bad. It's illegal."

Others, like Maggie, 15, learned the hard way. Four months ago, she thought she was going to die after she smoked $200 worth of primos and took three LSD tabs in the span of two hours.

Maggie, who began taking drugs when she was 12 because "I just wanted to see how it felt to get high," entered a hospital drug-rehab program after the incident and has remained drug-free.

"You do drugs because you want to, not because anybody makes you," Maggie says.

"Everybody thinks that marijuana is not a bad drug. But I tripped out on it, almost died. You hear from kids that 'it will never happen to me.' I used to think like that. My friends say that I'm going to go back to drugs. I'm not going to sit here and say that I'm going to stay drug-free the rest of my life because I don't know the future. But I do want to change."

Dennis, 15, a 10th-grader at John Marshall High School, says he knows marijuana is "dangerous stuff" because his parents have told him so. He says his friends who smoke pot and take other illicit drugs know that "it's bad for them, but they don't care about the consequences until it's too late. They don't listen to anybody. I'm tired that everyone is doing it."

So is Melissa, 17, a senior at Garfield High School, who says that kids smoke in the restrooms and at a nearby fast-food restaurant during lunchtime, and that they ditch class to get high.

"I have never experimented with drugs," she says. "My friends who do drugs don't act the same way. They were nicer before drugs. You could have a normal conversation with them, and now the only thing they talk about is acid and marijuana. Even the people you'd never imagine doing it are doing it—student leaders, students involved in school activities and sports. A lot of them do it because they are too stressed out."

"It's the '90s"

For some "good" kids, the temptation is hard to resist.

Jesse, a 17-year-old college-bound senior, athlete and straight-A student at an Eastside high school, says he drinks beer and smokes weed just about every weekend because it's the social thing and "it makes you less shy. It's a way to unwind.

"When the weekend comes, I don't want to think about my homework. I don't want to think about football practice. I wanna party."

And partying almost always includes excessive beer guzzling and drinking a mixture of punch with whiskey and vodka—and smoking bud.

"My parents are smart and everything," he says, "but they think that we are just going to a party to talk. If there's a party and there's no weed and no beer, no one goes.

"A lot of people think that it's just low-life and troubled kids who drink and do weed. But it is not," Jesse says. "Us, the ones who are college bound, we know that we're not going to be smoking pot all our lives and drinking. It's a sign of the times. Everyone is doing it. It's fun. It's the '90s."

"One of marihuana's greatest
advantages as a medicine is its
remarkable safety."

MARIJUANA IS NOT HARMFUL

Lester Grinspoon, James B. Bakalar, John P. Morgan,
and Lynn Zimmer

In Part I of the following two-part viewpoint, Lester Grinspoon
and James P. Bakalar argue that marijuana offers many health
benefits, especially for people suffering from the discomfort and
pain of diseases such as cancer, AIDS, and glaucoma. Grinspoon
and Bakalar advocate easing the restrictions on the medical use
of marijuana. In Part II, John P. Morgan and Lynn Zimmer refute
the argument that marijuana use leads to the abuse of hard-core
drugs. Grinspoon and Bakalar are the authors of the book *Marihuana, the Forbidden Medicine*. Morgan and Zimmer are on the board
of directors of NORML, the National Organization for the Reform of Marijuana Laws, which works to legalize marijuana.

As you read, consider the following questions:

1. What are some specific health benefits of marijuana,
   according to Grinspoon and Bakalar?
2. What evidence do Morgan and Zimmer give to support their
   argument that marijuana is not a gateway drug?
3. Why do the Dutch consider their marijuana laws successful
   even though more Dutch teenagers use marijuana now than
   in the past, according to Morgan and Zimmer?

I

Between 1840 and 1900, European and American medical journals published more than 100 articles on the therapeutic use of the drug known then as *Cannabis indica* (or Indian hemp) and now as marihuana. It was recommended as an appetite stimulant, muscle relaxant, analgesic, hypnotic, and anticonvulsant. As late as 1913 Sir William Osler recommended it as the most satisfactory remedy for migraine.

Today the 5000-year medical history of cannabis has been almost forgotten. Its use declined in the early 20th century because the potency of preparations was variable, responses to oral ingestion were erratic, and alternatives became available—injectable opiates and, later, synthetic drugs such as aspirin and barbiturates. In the United States, the final blow was struck by the Marihuana Tax Act of 1937. Designed to prevent nonmedical use, this law made cannabis so difficult to obtain for medical purposes that it was removed from the pharmacopeia. It is now confined to Schedule I under the Controlled Substances Act as a drug that has a high potential for abuse, lacks an accepted medical use, and is unsafe for use under medical supervision.

In 1972 the National Organization for the Reform of Marijuana Laws petitioned the Bureau of Narcotics and Dangerous Drugs, later renamed the Drug Enforcement Administration (DEA), to transfer marihuana to Schedule II so that it could be legally prescribed. As the proceedings continued, other parties joined, including the Physicians Association for AIDS [acquired immunodeficiency syndrome] Care. It was only in 1986, after many years of legal maneuvering, that the DEA acceded to the demand for the public hearings required by law. During the hearings, which lasted 2 years, many patients and physicians testified and thousands of pages of documentation were introduced. In 1988 the DEA's own administrative law judge, Francis L. Young, declared that marihuana in its natural form fulfilled the legal requirement of currently accepted medical use in treatment in the United States. He added that it was "one of the safest therapeutically active substances known to man." His order that the marihuana plant be transferred to Schedule II was overruled, not by any medical authority, but by the DEA itself, which issued a final rejection of all pleas for reclassification in March 1992.

BUREAUCRATIC BURDEN

Meanwhile, a few patients have been able to obtain marihuana legally for therapeutic purposes. Since 1978, legislation permitting patients with certain disorders to use marihuana with a physician's approval has been enacted in 36 states. Although federal regulations and procedures made the laws difficult to implement, 10 states eventually established formal marihuana research programs to seek Food and Drug Administration (FDA) approval for Investigational New Drug (IND) applications. These programs were later abandoned, mainly because the bureaucratic burden on physicians and patients became intolerable.

Growing demand also forced the FDA to institute an Individual Treatment IND (commonly referred to as a Compassionate IND) for the use of physicians whose patients needed marihuana because no other drug would produce the same therapeutic effect. The application process was made enormously complicated, and most physicians did not want to become involved, especially since many believed there was some stigma attached to prescribing cannabis. Between 1976 and 1988 the government reluctantly awarded about a half dozen Compassionate INDs for the use of marihuana. In 1989 the FDA was deluged with new applications from people with AIDS, and the number granted rose to 34 within a year. In June 1991, the Public Health Service announced that the program would be suspended because it undercut the administration's opposition to the use of illegal drugs. After that no new Compassionate INDs were granted, and the program was discontinued in March 1992. Eight patients are still receiving marihuana under the original program; for everyone else it is officially a forbidden medicine.

EFFECTIVE AND SAFE

And yet physicians and patients in increasing numbers continue to relearn through personal experience the lessons of the 19th century. Many people know that marihuana is now being used illegally for the nausea and vomiting induced by chemotherapy. Some know that it lowers intraocular pressure in glaucoma. Patients have found it useful as an anticonvulsant, as a muscle relaxant in spastic disorders, and as an appetite stimulant in the wasting syndrome of human immunodeficiency virus infection. It is also being used to relieve phantom limb pain, menstrual cramps, and other types of chronic pain, including (as Osler might have predicted) migraine. Polls and voter referenda have repeatedly indicated that the vast majority of Americans think marihuana should be medically available.

One of marihuana's greatest advantages as a medicine is its remarkable safety. It has little effect on major physiological functions. There is no known case of a lethal overdose; on the basis of animal models, the ratio of lethal to effective dose is estimated as 40,000 to 1. By comparison, the ratio is between 3 and 50 to 1 for secobarbital and between 4 and 10 to 1 for ethanol. Marihuana is also far less addictive and far less subject to abuse than many drugs now used as muscle relaxants, hypnotics, and analgesics. The chief legitimate concern is the effect of smoking on the lungs. Cannabis smoke carries even more tars and other particulate matter than tobacco smoke. But the amount smoked is much less, especially in medical use, and once marihuana is an openly recognized medicine, solutions may be found. Water pipes are a partial answer; ultimately a technology for the inhalation of cannabinoid vapors could be developed. Even if smoking continued, legal availability would make it easier to take precautions against aspergilli and other pathogens. At present, the greatest danger in medical use of marihuana is its illegality, which imposes much anxiety and expense on suffering people, forces them to bargain with illicit drug dealers, and exposes them to the threat of criminal prosecution.

THE CASE FOR REPEAL OF PROHIBITION

Of all the drugs that are currently illicit, marijuana perhaps presents the easiest case for repeal of the prohibition laws, in good part because it presents relatively few serious risks to users and is less dangerous in most respects than both alcohol and tobacco. Moreover, the available evidence indicates no apparent increase in marijuana use following the decriminalization of marijuana possession in about a dozen states during the late 1970s. In the Netherlands, which went even further during the 1970s in relaxing enforcement of marijuana laws, some studies indicate use of the drug has actually declined.

Ethan A. Nadelmann, Foreign Policy, Spring 1988.

The main active substance in cannabis, Δ^9-tetrahydrocannabinol (Δ^9-THC), has been available for limited purposes as a Schedule II synthetic drug since 1985. This medicine, dronabinol (Marinol), taken orally in capsule form, is sometimes said to obviate the need for medical marihuana. Patients and physicians who have tried both disagree. The dosage and duration of action of marihuana are easier to control, and other cannabinoids in the marihuana plant may modify the action of Δ^9-THC. The development of cannabinoids in pure form should certainly be encouraged, but the time and resources required are great and at present unavailable. In these circumstances, further isolation, testing, and development of individual cannabinoids should not be considered a substitute for meeting the immediate needs of suffering people.

Although it is often objected that the medical usefulness of marihuana has not been demonstrated by controlled studies, several informal experiments involving large numbers of subjects suggest an advantage for marihuana over oral Δ^9-THC and other medicines. For example, from 1978 through 1986 the state research program in New Mexico provided marihuana or synthetic Δ^9-THC to about 250 cancer patients receiving chemotherapy after conventional medications failed to control their nausea and vomiting. A physician who worked with the program testified at a DEA hearing that for these patients marihuana was clearly superior to both chlorpromazine and synthetic Δ^9-THC. It is true that we do not have studies controlled according to the standards required by the FDA—chiefly because legal, bureaucratic, and financial obstacles are constantly put in the way. The situation is ironical, since so much research has been done on marihuana, often in unsuccessful attempts to prove its dangerous and addictive character, that we know more about it than about most prescription drugs. . . .

PHYSICIANS MUST ACT

The American Medical Association was one of the few organizations that raised a voice in opposition to the Marihuana Tax Act of 1937, yet today most physicians seem to take little active interest in the subject, and their silence is often cited by those who are determined that marihuana shall remain a forbidden medicine. Meanwhile, many physicians pretend to ignore the fact that their patients with cancer, AIDS, or multiple sclerosis are smoking marihuana for relief; some quietly encourage them. In a 1990 survey, 44% of oncologists said they had suggested that a patient smoke marihuana for relief of the nausea induced by chemotherapy. If marihuana were actually unsafe for use even under medical supervision, as its Schedule I status explicitly affirms, this recommendation would be unthinkable. It is time for physicians to acknowledge more openly that the present classification is scientifically, legally, and morally wrong.

Physicians have both a right and a duty to be skeptical about therapeutic claims for any substance, but only after putting aside fears and doubts connected with the stigma of illicit nonmedical drug use. Advocates of medical use of marihuana are sometimes charged with using medicine as a wedge to open a way for "recreational" use. The accusation is false as applied to its target, but expresses in a distorted form a truth about some opponents of medical marihuana: they will not admit that it can be a safe and effective medicine largely because they are stubbornly committed to exaggerating its dangers when used for nonmedical purposes.

We are not asking readers for immediate agreement with our affirmation that marihuana is medically useful, but we hope they will do more to encourage open and legal exploration of its potential. The ostensible indifference of physicians should no longer be used as a justification for keeping this medicine in the shadows.

II

The Partnership for a Drug-Free America, in cooperation with the National Institute on Drug Abuse (NIDA) and the White House Office of Drug Control Policy, recently announced a new anti-drug campaign that specifically targets marijuana. Instead of featuring horror tales of marijuana-induced insanity, violence, and birth defects, this campaign is built upon the premise that reducing marijuana use is a practical strategy for reducing the use of more dangerous drugs.

The primary basis for this "gateway hypothesis" is a report by the Center on Addiction and Substance Abuse (CASA) claiming that marijuana users are 85 times more likely than non-marijuana users to try cocaine. This figure, using data from NIDA's 1991 National Household Survey on Drug Abuse, is close to being meaningless. It was calculated by dividing the proportion of marijuana users who have ever used cocaine (17%) by the proportion of cocaine users who have never used marijuana (0.2%). The high risk factor obtained is a product not of the fact that so many marijuana users use cocaine, but that so many cocaine users used marijuana previously.

It is hardly a revelation that people who use one of the least popular drugs are likely to use the more popular ones—not only marijuana, but also alcohol and tobacco cigarettes. The obvious statistic not publicized by CASA is that most marijuana users (83%) *never used cocaine*. Indeed, for nearly 70 million Americans who have tried marijuana, it is clearly a "terminus" rather than a "gateway" drug.

No Link

During the last few years and after a decade of decline, there has been a slight increase in marijuana use particularly among youth. In 1994, 38% of high school seniors reported having ever tried the drug compared to about 35% in 1993 and 33% in 1992. This increase does not constitute a crisis. No one knows whether marijuana use-rates will continue to rise. But even if they do, it will not necessarily lead to increased use of cocaine.

Since the 1970s, when NIDA first began gathering data, rates of marijuana and cocaine use have displayed divergent patterns. Marijuana prevalence increased throughout the 1970s, peaking in 1979 when about 60% of high school seniors reported having used it at least once. During the 1980s, cocaine use increased while marijuana use was declining. Since 1991, when data for the CASA analysis was gathered, marijuana use-rates have increased while cocaine use-rates have remained fairly steady.

This over-changing nature of the statistical relationship between use-rates for marijuana and cocaine indicates the *absence* of a causal link between the use of these two drugs. Therefore, even if the proposed Partnership campaign were to be effective in reducing marijuana use it would not guarantee a proportional reduction in the number of people who use cocaine. To the extent anti-drug campaigns are effective, they seem to be most effective in deterring those people who would have only been fairly low-level users. There is no reason to believe that anti-marijuana messages of any sort would deter many of those marijuana users—currently 17% of the total—who also develop an interest in cocaine.

ANTI-DRUG MESSAGES ARE INEFFECTIVE

Nor is there reason to believe that the Partnership's new campaign will actually reduce the overall number of marijuana users. For a decade now, American youth have been subjected to an unparalleled assault of anti-drug messages. They have seen hundreds of Partnership advertisements on television and in print media. They have been urged to "just say no" by rock stars, sports heroes, presidents, and first ladies. They have been exposed to anti-drug educational programs in the schools. Yet this is the same generation of young people that recently began increasing its use of marijuana. If seems unlikely that many of them will be deterred by hyperbolic claims of marijuana's gateway effect, particularly when it contradicts the reality of drug use they see around them.

If the creators of American drug policy are truly interested in reducing the risk of marijuana users using other drugs, then they should take a closer look at Holland—a nation whose drug policy since the 1970s has been guided by a commitment to diminishing any potential gateway effect. Wanting to keep young marijuana users away from cocaine and other "hard drugs," the Dutch decided to separate the retail markets by allowing anyone 18 years of age or older to purchase marijuana openly in government-controlled "coffee shops" which strictly prohibit the use and sale of other drugs.

A SUCCESSFUL POLICY

Despite easy availability, marijuana prevalence among 12- to 18-year-olds in Holland is only 13.6%—well below the 38% use-rate for American high school seniors. More Dutch teenagers use marijuana now than in the past; indeed, lifetime prevalence increased nearly three-fold between 1984 and 1992, from 4.8% to 13.6%. However, Dutch officials consider their policy a success because the increase in marijuana use has not been accompanied by an increase in the use of other drugs. For the last decade, the rate of cocaine use among Dutch youth has remained stable, with about 0.3% of 12- to 18-year-olds reporting having used it in the past month.

In the United States, the claim that marijuana acts as a gateway to the use of other drugs serves mainly as a rhetorical tool for frightening Americans into believing that winning the war against heroin and cocaine requires waging a battle against the casual use of marijuana. Not only is the claim intellectually indefensible, but the battle is wasteful of resources and fated to failure.

46

PERIODICAL BIBLIOGRAPHY

The following articles have been selected to supplement the diverse views presented in this chapter. Addresses are provided for periodicals not indexed in the *Readers' Guide to Periodical Literature*, the *Alternative Press Index*, the *Social Sciences Index*, or the *Index to Legal Periodicals and Books*.

Robert I. Block	"Does Heavy Marijuana Use Impair Human Cognition and Brain Function?" *JAMA*, February 21, 1996. Available from AMA, Library, 515 N. State St., Chicago, IL 60610.
Marilyn Chase	"Beneficial Drinking: After Abstinence, Before Tying One On," *Wall Street Journal*, July 3, 1995.
Trip Gabriel	"Heroin Finds a New Market Along Cutting Edge of Style," *New York Times*, May 8, 1994.
William Grimes	"Good News on Drinking; Fries with That, Please," *New York Times*, January 7, 1996.
Steve Hochman	"Heroin: Back on the Charts," *Rolling Stone*, September 27, 1992.
Mark A.R. Kleiman and Jonathan P. Caulkins	"Heroin Policy for the Next Decade," *Annals of the American Academy of Political and Social Science*, May 1992.
Mara Leveritt	"Pot's Not So Bad," *NORML's Active Resistance*, Spring 1995. Available from NORML, 2001 S St. NW, Suite 640, Washington, DC 20009.
Mark Miller	"Fatal Addiction," *Mademoiselle*, November 1991.
Ethan Nadelman and Jennifer McNeely	"Doing Methadone Right," *Public Interest*, Spring 1996.
Harrison G. Pope and Deborah Yurgelun-Todd	"The Residual Cognitive Effects of Heavy Marijuana Use in College Students," *JAMA*, February 21, 1996.
Marc A. Schuckit	"Alcohol Dependence in Women: Is It Really Unique?" *Drug Abuse & Alcoholism Newsletter*, February 1995. Available from Vista Hill Foundation, 2355 Northside Dr., 3rd Fl., San Diego, CA 92108.
Marc A. Schuckit	"Does Marijuana Have Any Medicinal Value?" *Drug Abuse & Alcoholism Newsletter*, April 1996.
Ronald G. Victor and Jim Hansen	"Alcohol and Blood Pressure," *New England Journal of Medicine*, June 29, 1995. Available from 1440 Main St., Waltham, MA 02254.

CHAPTER

2

WHAT CAUSES
CHEMICAL
DEPENDENCY?

CHAPTER PREFACE

Some people can drink or use drugs and never become addicted. Others quickly become addicted and never overcome their addiction. Why people differ in their tendency toward addiction is one of the questions researchers are trying to answer in their search for understanding the causes of and solutions to chemical dependency.

Researchers are exploring several factors in their attempts to understand addiction: the physical craving for a substance, the psychological need to continue a habit, and the social environment that might encourage or discourage the use of a substance. The importance of each factor varies depending on the substance used and the individual involved.

For example, heroin is highly addictive physically—the body becomes accustomed to the heroin, and if use is suddenly stopped the addict endures a very painful physical withdrawal. Cocaine, on the other hand, is less physically addictive but extremely psychologically addictive—the high from cocaine is so pleasurable that laboratory animals will choose cocaine over food until they overdose or starve to death. Almost all drugs have a social component to them; that is, the people and/or the society around an addict often encourage the use of the substance.

Most experts believe that a typical addict may have numerous factors influencing his or her tendency toward addiction. For example, an alcoholic may have a genetic disposition toward alcoholism, may use alcohol for psychological reasons, and may be surrounded by friends and family who use alcohol socially. All of these factors combined make it very difficult for the alcoholic to find a treatment that will address all of these causes and enable him or her to stop drinking.

In the following chapter, the authors present a variety of causes for chemical dependency. They discuss why some individuals are more prone to addiction than others and present some ideas on how to address the various causes of addiction.

| *"Addiction is a chronic, relapsing disease."*

CHEMICAL DEPENDENCY IS A DISEASE

U.S. Department of Health and Human Services

The U.S. Department of Health and Human Services (HHS) is the division of the federal government that administers health and social security programs. In the following viewpoint, excerpted from a report by HHS, the authors state that addiction to chemicals—whether illegal drugs, legal drugs, or alcohol—is a potentially life-threatening disease. The authors write that addiction has physiological and behavioral components similar to other diseases and that it can result in severe damage to the human body and to society in general. Although no cure exists for addiction, according to HHS, it can be treated successfully.

As you read, consider the following questions:

1. What percentage of American adults and adolescents are affected by addiction, according to HHS?
2. What are the effects of addiction, in the authors' view?
3. What are the symptoms of addiction, according to the authors?

From U.S. Department of Health and Human Services, "Effectiveness of Substance Abuse Treatment," white paper, pp. 1-5, September 1995.

Despite considerable public discussion of the devastating consequences of alcohol and other drug addiction, misconceptions persist about addiction and its treatment. This viewpoint summarizes the fundamental facts that have emerged over decades of research and practice. . . .

Substance abuse is a problem affecting all sectors of American society. It crosses all societal boundaries, in both urban and rural areas. It affects both genders, every ethnic group, and people in every tax bracket.

Today, we know that:

• Addiction is a chronic, relapsing disease that, like hypertension or diabetes, has roots in both genetic susceptibility and personal behavior;

• Although addiction has no known "cure," it can be controlled through treatment;

• Treatment for addiction is effective and becoming more so; and

• The costs of untreated addiction—violence and other crime, poor health, family breakup and other social ills—far exceed the costs of addiction treatment.

No One Intends to Become Addicted

Addiction is a common, potentially life threatening, chronic disease that affects approximately 10 percent of American adults and 3 percent of adolescents. Biological predispositions, psychological and social factors lead to alcohol and other drug problems, despite serious consequences and individuals' desire to abstain.

It seems certain that no one experiments with alcohol and other drugs with the intention of becoming addicted. Although addictive drugs can produce intense and immediate pleasure, or reduce extreme anxiety, the price of pain the addict eventually pays is exacted more gradually.

The roots of addiction are both organic and environmental. Like hypertension, atherosclerosis, adult diabetes and other medical conditions, addiction is caused by genetic predisposition, social circumstances and such personal behaviors as sedentary lifestyle, poor eating habits and uncontrolled stress. Interpersonal relationships also have an impact on substance use and abuse.

Certain drugs are highly addictive, rapidly causing biochemical and structural changes in the brain. Others can be used for longer periods of time before they begin to cause inescapable cravings and compulsive use. Some individuals have a greater tendency toward addiction than others. People with addictive disorders seek out alcohol and other drugs and use them compulsively, often in spite of their own best interests and intentions.

DRY, NOT SOBER

Addiction and alcoholism are diseases. Addicts and alcoholics who are forced to abstain from their drug of choice due, say, to imprisonment or threat thereof are, in the nomenclature of the field, "dry" rather than "sober." They are still addicts and alcoholics. . . . The overwhelming majority will sooner or later . . . return to drugs or alcohol.

Daniel K. Benjamin and Roger Leroy Miller, *Undoing Drugs: Beyond Legalization*, 1991.

Addictive drugs wreak havoc on the body, attacking the liver, the lungs, the heart and the brain. As a result, although many addicts are able to hold jobs and maintain some semblance of normal lives, in the long term, all drugs of addiction have toxic effects—on the addicted individuals, their families, their communities, and on society as a whole. Addictive use also opens the door to infectious diseases including tuberculosis, hepatitis and HIV/AIDS.

EFFECTS OF ADDICTION

Like a malignancy, the effects of addiction spread to the entire social body, contributing to violence and crime, child abuse and neglect, homelessness and other social ills. The economic costs associated with alcohol and other drug problems are truly staggering; $165.5 billion in 1990.

For example, without treatment, alcoholics spend twice as much on health care as people without alcohol problems. Approximately half the cost of alcohol and other drug abuse treatment is offset within one year of subsequent reductions in the use of medical services by the affected family, not just the primary patient. Two years after substance abuse treatment, one study documents a 40% reduction in health care costs to participants.

Addiction has no known "cure," but many well-documented treatments can reverse or contain its devastating effects.

Addiction is a debilitating condition with physical and mental causes and consequences. Diagnostic criteria for addiction, agreed upon by the American Psychiatric Association and the World Health Organization, include physical effects, such as marked tolerance and symptoms of withdrawal, and psychological consequences, including craving and a mental focus on obtaining and using drugs. Addiction fuels destructive behavior patterns that are exceedingly difficult to break.

Many Americans are in a "middle ground," not technically "addicted" but clearly having a problem. Anyone who regularly uses a mind-altering drug and finds it difficult to stop, even those who may not be "addicted," can benefit from substance abuse treatment.

Some individuals are able to stop using alcohol and other drugs on their own, with the assistance of family, friends, or other members of their community. Many more, however, need the help of specialized counseling, support and/or medical therapies. People with alcohol and other drug problems may also have underlying psychiatric conditions, such as depression or schizophrenia, which also must be diagnosed and treated.

Substance abuse treatment programs differ in philosophy, setting, duration, and approach. Most involve some combination of detoxification, rehabilitation, continuing care (often called "aftercare") and relapse prevention. Individuals may move through each of these phases more than once, revisiting certain activities as part of their recovery. The idea of a continuum of services is very important, where treatment is seen as an ongoing process involving several different but essential components. As in other areas of medical treatment, there are several different "levels of care" which allow individuals to be treated at the most appropriate level of intensity.

"Nature gave us the ability to become
hooked because the brain has clearly
evolved a reward system."

BIOLOGICAL FACTORS CONTRIBUTE
TO CHEMICAL DEPENDENCY

Joann Ellison Rodgers

Joann Ellison Rodgers is deputy director of public affairs and director of media relations for the Johns Hopkins Medical Institutions. She is also president of the Council for the Advancement
of Science Writing, a lecturer in the department of epidemiology at the Johns Hopkins School of Hygiene and Public Health,
and the author of numerous books and articles on medical issues. In the following viewpoint, Rodgers writes that researchers
have concluded that chemical dependency is not a disease or
character flaw but a complex behavior that is driven largely by
natural chemical processes in the brain.

As you read, consider the following questions:
1. Why does the brain have "reward" circuits, according to
   Rodgers?
2. What is wrong with the disease model of addiction, in the
   author's opinion?
3. What are the most common characteristics of addictions that
   burden society, according to Rodgers?

Millions of Americans are apparently "hooked," not only on heroin, morphine, amphetamines, tranquilizers, and cocaine, but also nicotine, caffeine, sugar, steroids, work, theft, gambling, exercise, and even love and sex. The War on Drugs alone is older than the century. From 1990 to 1994, the United States spent $45 billion waging it, with no end in sight, despite every kind of addiction treatment from psychosurgery, psychoanalysis, psychedelics, and self-help to acupuncture, group confrontation, family therapy, hypnosis, meditation, education, and tough love.

There seems no end to our "dependencies," their bewildering intractability, the glib explanations for their causes and even more glib "solutions."

The news, however, is that brain, mind, and behavior specialists are rethinking the whole notion of addiction. With help from neuroscience, molecular biology, pharmacology, psychology, and genetics, they're challenging their own hard-core assumptions and popular "certainties" and finding surprisingly common characteristics among addictions.

They're using new imaging techniques to see how addiction looks and feels and where cravings "live" in the brain and mind. They're concluding that things are far from hopeless and they are rapidly replacing conjecture with facts.

ADDICTION IS NATURAL

For example, scientists have learned that every animal, from the ancient hagfish to reptiles, rodents, and humans, shares the same basic pleasure and "reward" circuits in the brain, circuits that all turn on when in contact with addictive substances or during pleasurable acts such as eating or orgasm. One conclusion from this evidence is that addictive behaviors are normal, a natural part of our "wiring." If they weren't, or if they were rare, nature would not have let the capacity to be addicted evolve, survive, and stick around in every living creature.

"Everyone engages in addictive behaviors to some extent because such things as eating, drinking, and sex are essential to survival and highly reinforcing," says G. Alan Marlatt, Ph.D., director of the Addictive Behaviors Research Center at the University of Washington. "We get immediate gratification from them and find them very hard to give up indeed. That's a pretty good definition of addiction."

"The inescapable fact is that nature gave us the ability to become hooked because the brain has clearly evolved a reward system, just as it has a pain system," says physiologist and pharmacologist Steven Childers, Ph.D., of Bowman Gray School of Medicine in North Carolina. "The fact that some things may accidentally or inadvertently trigger that system is somewhat beside the point.

"Our brains didn't develop opiate receptors to tempt us with heroin addiction. The coca plant didn't develop cocaine to produce what we call crack addicts. This plant doesn't care two hoots about our brain. But heroin and cocaine addiction certainly tell us a great deal about how brains work. And how they work is that if you taste or experience something that you like, that feels good, you're reinforced to do that again. Basic drives, for food, sex, and pleasure, activate reward centers in the brain. They're part of human nature."

NEW THINKING, OLD PROBLEM

What we now call "addictions," in this sense, Childers says, are cases of a good and useful phenomenon taken hostage, with terrible social and medical consequences. Moreover, that insight is leading to the identification of specific areas of the brain that link feelings and behavior to reward circuits. "In the case of addictive drugs, we know that areas of the brain involved in memory and learning and with the most ancient part of our brain, the emotional brain, are the most interesting. I'm very optimistic that we will be able to develop new strategies for preventing and treating addictions."

The new concept of addiction is in sharp contrast to the conventional, frustrating, and some would say cynical view that everything causes addiction.

Ask 10 Americans what addiction is and what causes it and you might get at least 10 answers. Some will insist addiction is a failure of morality or a spiritual weakness, a sin and a crime by people who won't take responsibility for their behavior. If addicts want to self-destruct, let them. It's their fault; they choose to abuse.

For the teetotaler and politicians, it's a self-control problem; for sociologists, poverty; for educators, ignorance. Ask some psychiatrists or psychologists and you're told that personality traits, temperament, and "character" are at the root of addictive "personalities." Social-learning and cognitive-behavior theorists will tell you it's a case of conditioned response and intended or unintended reinforcement of inappropriate behaviors. The biologically oriented will say it's all in the genes and heredity; anthropologists that it's culturally determined. . . .

The most popular "theory," however, is that addictive behaviors are diseases. In this view, an addict, like a cancer patient or a diabetic, either has it or does not have it. Popularized by Alcoholics Anonymous, the disease theory holds that addictions are irreversible, constitutional, and altogether abnormal and that the only appropriate treatment is total avoidance of the alcohol or other substance, lifelong abstinence, and constant vigilance.

The problem with all of these theories and models is that they lead to control measures doomed to failure by mixing up the process of addiction with its impact. Worse, from the scientific standpoint, they don't hold up to the tests of observation, time, and consistent utility. They don't explain much and they don't account for a lot. . . .

DEBUNKING THE DOMINO THEORY

"I began to understand the bankruptcy of many addiction theories when a lot of my predictions about alcoholism and treatment for it were dead wrong," says William R. Miller, Ph.D. A professor of psychology and psychiatry and director of the Center on Alcoholism, Substance Abuse, and Addictions at the University of New Mexico, his controversial studies of "controlled drinking" in the early 1970s were among the first to clash with the "disease" theory of addictions.

"I developed a reasonably successful program that taught alcoholics how to drink moderately. Lots of them eventually totally quit and became abstainers. I would never have predicted that. The prevalent theories were that they would either eventually relapse and lose control of their drinking or that they would quit because moderation did not work. We knew from blood and urine tests that they were able to moderate but quit anyhow. The old domino theory that one drink equals a drunk proved, for some, to be baloney. We know with cigarette smoking and alcohol and other addictive behaviors that moderation, tapering, and 'warm turkey' can be very effective." Miller blames mostly the persistent strength of the addiction-as-disease concept on the peculiarly American experience with alcohol and Prohibition.

"During Prohibition, alcohol was marked as completely dangerous and the message was that no one could use it safely. At the end of Prohibition, we had a problem: a cognitive dissonance. Clearly many people could use it safely, so we needed a new model to make drinking permissible again. That led to the idea that only 'some' people can't handle it, those who have a disease called alcoholism."

Everyone likes this model, Miller says. People with alcohol problems like it because they get special status as victims of a disease and get treatment. Nonalcoholics like it because they can tell themselves they don't need to worry if they don't have the "disease." The treatment industry loves it because there's money to be made, and the liquor industry loves it because under this theory, it's not alcohol that's the problem but the alcoholic.

"What's really bizarre," says Miller, "is that the alcohol beverage industry spends a lot of money to help teach us about the disease model. It's the inverse of the temperance movement, which many now laugh at, but which saw alcohol more realistically as a dangerous drug. It is."

Today, Miller notes, heroin and cocaine are looked upon the way the temperance movement once looked on alcohol. "Ironically, too," he says, "we are treating nicotine and gluttony the way we once treated alcohol. It's easy to see how the disease model and all other single-cause theories of addiction can lead to blind alleys and bad treatments in which therapists adopt every fad and reach into a bulging bag of tricks for whatever is in hand or intuitively meets the immediate moment. But what we wind up with are three myths about alcoholism and other addictions: that nothing works, that one particular approach is superior to all others, and that everything works about equally well. That's nonsense."

NO EASY TARGETS

"The most likely truth about addiction is that it's not a single, basic mechanism, but several problems we label 'addiction,'" says Michael F. Cataldo, Ph.D., chief of behavioral psychology at Johns Hopkins Medical Institutes. "No one thing explains addiction," echoes Miller. "There are things about individuals, about the environment in which they live, and about the substances involved that must be factored in." Experts today prefer the term "addictive behaviors," rather than addiction, to underscore their belief that while everyone has the capacity for addiction, it's what people do that should drive treatment.

So while all addictions display common properties, the proportions of those factors vary widely. And certainly not all addictions have the same effect on the quality of our lives or capacity to be dangerous. Everyday bad habits, compulsions, dependencies, and cravings clearly have something in common with heroin and cocaine addiction, in terms of their mechanisms and triggers. But what about people who are Type A personalities; who eat chocolate every day; who, like Microsoft's Bill Gates, focus almost pathologically on work; who feel compelled to expose themselves in public, seek thrills like race-car driving and fire fighting, or obsess constantly over hand washing, hair twirling, or playing video games. They have—from the standpoint of what their behavior actually means to themselves and others—very little in common with heroin and crack addicts.

ADDICTED TO LOVE

Or consider two of the more fascinating candidates for addiction—sex and love. Anthropologist Helen Fisher, Ph.D., of the American Museum of Natural History, suggests that the initial rush of arousal and romantic, erotic love, the "chemistry" that hooks a couple to each other, produces effects in the brain parallel to what happens when a brain is exposed to morphine or amphetamines.

In the case of love, the reactions involve chemicals such as endorphins, the brain's own opiates, and oxytocin and vasopressin, naturally occurring hormones linked to male and female bonding. After a while, though, this effect diminishes as the brain's receptor sites for these chemicals become overloaded and thus desensitized. Tolerance occurs; attachment wanes and sets up the mind for separation, so that the "addicted" man or woman is ready to pursue the high elsewhere. In this scenario, divorce or adultery becomes the equivalent of drug-seeking behavior, addicts craving for the high. According to Fisher, the fact that most people stay married is "a triumph of culture over nature," much the way, perhaps, nonaddiction is.

COMMON CHARACTERISTICS OF ADDICTION

Experts generally agree on the most common characteristics of addictions that trouble society:

• The substance or activity that triggers them must initially cause feelings of pleasure and changes in emotion or mood.

• The body develops a physical tolerance to the substance or activity so that addicts must take ever-larger amounts to get the same effects.

• Removal of the drug or activity causes painful withdrawal symptoms.

• Quite apart from physical tolerance, addiction involves physical and psychological dependence associated with craving that is independent of the need to avoid the pain of withdrawal.

• Addiction always causes changes in the brain and mind. These include physiological changes, chemical changes, anatomical changes, and behavioral changes.

• Addiction requires a prior experience with a substance or behavior. The first contact with the substance or activity is an initiation that may or may not lead to addiction, but must occur in order to set in motion the effects in the brain that are likely to encourage a person to try that experience again.

• Addictions cause repeated behavioral problems, take a lot of a person's time and energy, are openly sanctioned by the community, and are marked by a gradual obsession with the drug or behavior.

• Addictions develop their own motivations. For addicts, their tolerance and dependence in and of themselves become reinforcing and rewarding, independent of their actual use of the drug or the "high" they may get. "One way of understanding this," says Cataldo, "is to analyze what is happening behaviorally in withdrawal. Given that withdrawal is so punishing, why do addicts let themselves go through it more than once? One answer is that the withdrawal, when combined with relapse and returning to the use of the substance, itself may be 'rewarding.'"

HAIR OF THE DOG

The withdrawal and relapse cycle suggests that like any behavior, the addict "gets something out of" the pain of withdrawal—attention, perhaps, or help. But, in any case, enough so that he not only is willing to do it again, but also may seek out the cycle the way he once sought out the drug.

In gambling addictions and certain eating disorders, particularly, says Toni Farrenkopf, Ph.D., a Seattle psychologist, the "rush" for the addict often comes from pursuit of the activity after "getting clean and clear" for a while, along with eluding police, spouses, parents, bill collectors, and employers.

"We know this is the case with animals we can train to do something, even if they never get a positive reward out of it," Cataldo says. The "reward" is escape from or absence of an electric shock or punishment, even if it's only occasional escape or unpredictable escape. The cocaine addict may be addicted to the pursuit of cocaine and stealing to get money to buy the drug; using coke may be secondary to the reward of not getting caught and the "high" of pursuing the drug life-style.

If addictions have characteristics in common, so do addicts, the experts say.

They have particular vulnerabilities or susceptibilities, opportunity to have contact with the substance or activity that will addict them, and a risk of relapse no matter how successfully they are treated. They tend to be risk takers and thrill seekers and expect to have a positive reaction to their substance of abuse before they use it.

Addicts have distinct preferences for one substance over another and for how they use the substance of abuse. They have problems with self-regulation and impulse control, tend to use drugs as a substitute for coping strategies in dealing with both stress and their everyday lives in general, and don't seek "escape" so much as a way to manage their lives. Finally, addicts tend to have higher-than-normal capacity for such drugs. Alcoholics, for example, often can drink friends "under the table" and appear somewhat normal, even drive (not safely) on doses of alcohol that would put most people to sleep or kill them.

MAINLY IN THE BRAIN

The biological, psychological, and social processes by which addictions occur also have common pathways, but with complicated loops and detours. All addictions appear now to have roots in genetic susceptibilities and biological traits. But like all human and animal behaviors, including eating, sleeping, and learning, addictive behavior takes a lot of handling. The end product is a bit like Mozart's talent: If he'd never come in contact with a piano or with music, it's unlikely he would have expressed his musical gifts.

Floyd E. Bloom, M.D., chairman of neuropharmacology at the Scripps Clinical and Research Foundation in La Jolla, California, once gave a talk called "The Bane of Pain Is Mainly in the Brain." His point was that both pain and pain relief occur in the brain, triggered by the release, control, uptake, and quantity of assorted brain chemicals and other natural substances. The same might be said for addiction. Regardless of the source of addiction, the effects are "mainly in the brain," physically, chemically, and psychologically affecting emotions and energy levels. . . .

PROMISING STRATEGIES

If there is a hitch in this new picture of addiction it is that it is far from simple. It is also politically incorrect, unlikely to make the "Just Say No" and "law and order" crowd very happy. But it is putting solid foundations under prevention and treatment programs and promising entirely new strategies to combat drug abuse. The implications of this new view of addiction are in fact profound for treatment, prevention, and public policy.

L.H.R. Drew, an Australian addiction expert, notes that "if the idea prevails that drug use—and more particularly drug addiction—is a special type of behavior which is highly contagious, irreversible, inevitably leads to disease, and is due to the special seductive properties of certain drugs, then our approach to reducing drug problems is not going to change. If, however, the ideas prevail that drug use is more similar than different to other behaviors and that there is little that is special about drug addiction compared with other addictions that are universally experienced, then the drug hysteria may abate and a rational approach to policies to reduce drug problems may be possible. It must be known that people get into trouble with drugs in the same way that they do with many other things . . . particularly behaviors giving short-term rewards."

In the new view of addiction, says Childers, people vary in their ability to manage problems and pleasures, "but we must recognize that we all share the same circuits of pleasure, rewards, and pain. Anyone who takes cocaine will enjoy it; anyone who has sex will enjoy it. There is nothing abnormal about getting high on cocaine. Everyone will. There is a natural basis of addiction and we need to get away from the concept that only bad or weak or diseased people have problems with addiction. Telling someone to 'just say no' is like telling someone to just say no to eating and drinking and sex. We must begin to see how very human and very hard this is. But it is far from hopeless."

"It is culture . . . that is the source of drinking problems."

CULTURAL FACTORS CONTRIBUTE TO CHEMICAL DEPENDENCY

Mona Charen

In the following viewpoint, Mona Charen disputes the theory that alcoholism is a disease and that the use of alcohol should be discouraged in order to prevent addiction. Charen argues that the abuse of alcohol is caused by cultural attitudes toward alcohol rather than by the addictive potential of alcohol itself. She contends that cultures that condone drunkenness are most likely to produce alcoholics. On the other hand, she writes, comparatively fewer alcoholics are found in cultures in which alcohol is associated with family and religious events and in which drunkenness is not tolerated. Charen is a nationally syndicated columnist.

As you read, consider the following questions:
1. What is the "medical model" of alcoholism, according to the author?
2. Why do many physicians hesitate to advise patients to drink alcohol for its health benefits, according to Charen?
3. What five steps does David Hanson recommend in order to curb problem drinking, as cited by Charen?

Mona Charen, "Tack on Alcohol May Be All Wet," *Washington Times*, June 15, 1995. Reprinted by permission of Mona Charen and Creators Syndicate.

Afther 40 years of hard drinking and cancer, Mickey Mantle's liver was shot.

Mantle had, in recent years, gotten his drinking under control. He did it in the prescribed American way—by accepting complete abstention for the rest of his life.

Almost all Americans now believe in the "medical model" of alcoholism. It is alcohol, we believe, that causes alcoholism. And alcoholism is a disease, like diabetes.

The way to prevent alcoholism, most Americans believe, is to stigmatize alcohol as a drug and discourage its use as strongly as possible. The Department of Education's drug and alcohol abuse materials are typical of the tone across the country. "Curricula which advocate responsible use of drugs (including alcohol) should be rejected."

WRONG ASSUMPTIONS

But it is quite possible, and I believe true, that our assumptions about alcohol and alcoholism are completely wrong. A slim little scholarly volume called *Preventing Alcohol Abuse*, by sociologist David Hanson of the State University of New York, challenges virtually every tenet of the modern American approach to alcohol.

Throughout our history, Americans—particularly those adhering to Protestant denominations—have viewed alcohol as evil. Since Prohibition, we've settled into the view that though alcohol is terrible, the social and economic costs of outlawing it are intolerably high. Other means of controlling consumption must therefore be found.

Mr. Hanson doesn't believe alcohol is evil. He believes that, used properly, it enhances life in many ways. Alcohol's health benefits, for example, reducing the risk of heart disease, are not in dispute among doctors. Where physicians differ is on whether to encourage patients to drink moderately. Many fear that such advice will inevitably lead to alcohol abuse.

DIFFERENT VIEWS OF ALCOHOL

Almost all human societies, throughout world history, have used alcohol. Mr. Hanson offers evidence that beer was fermented as early as 10,000 B.C. Throughout human history, alcohol offered medicinal, antiseptic and analgesic benefits. It was/is a social lubricant, a facilitator of relaxation and an aid to digestion.

Alcohol has also been abused by some since the dawn of civilization. But the severity and prevalence of alcohol abuse has differed dramatically in different societies. Some groups, like the Irish, have high rates of alcoholism and drunkenness; others, like Italians, Jews and Chinese, consume alcohol regularly with few pathological excesses.

Reviewing the scholarly literature, Mr. Hanson concludes that a society gets the behavior it tolerates—and expects. If the culture teaches that alcohol makes one convivial and friendly, then sexual advances and aggression are not found. But if the culture teaches the opposite, then aggression, sexual and otherwise, is likely to follow drinking. Experiments have shown that men given tonic water (but told it was gin and tonic) were more likely to act aggressively and sexually than those who were given vodka and told it was tonic.

PSYCHOLOGY OR PHYSIOLOGY?

A significant experiment conducted by Alan Marlatt of the University of Washington in Seattle and his colleagues in 1973 [showed] that alcoholics' drinking is correlated with their beliefs about alcohol and drinking. Marlatt successfully disguised beverages containing and not containing alcohol among a randomly assigned group of sixty-four alcoholic and social drinkers (the control group) asked to participate in a "taste-rating task." One group of subjects was given a beverage with alcohol but was told that although it tasted like alcohol it actually contained none. Subjects in another group were given a beverage with no alcohol (tonic) but were told that it did contain alcohol.

As Marlatt and co-authors reported in the *Journal of Abnormal Psychology*, they found "the consumption rates were higher in those conditions in which subjects were led to believe that they would consume alcohol, regardless of the actual beverage administered." The finding was obtained among both alcoholic and social drinker subjects. Marlatt's experiment suggests that according to their findings the ability of alcoholics to stop drinking alcohol is not determined by a physiological reaction to alcohol. A psychological fact—the belief that they were drinking alcohol—was operationally significant, not alcohol itself. . . .

These and similar studies support the idea that what goes on outside of a person's body is more significant in understanding drug use, including alcoholism, than what goes on inside the body.

Jeffrey A. Schaler, *Society*, September/October 1991.

Societies with low rates of alcohol abuse share certain features. Among Jews and Italians, for example, alcohol is introduced to children at an early age, is associated with family and religious events, and is not stigmatized. While drinking is regarded neutrally or positively, becoming drunk is treated harshly.

The Irish, by contrast, have a very different approach to alcohol. Drinking is done among men outside the home. It is not associated with food or religious rites. It is introduced as a rite of passage to adulthood. Moreover, being drunk is viewed indulgently and humorously. Indeed, the Irish are urged to "drown their sorrows" in drink.

"Forbidden Fruit"

Utter prohibition, such as that practiced by Mormons, is fraught with danger as well. A study of college students found that Mormons who do drink are far more likely to get drunk regularly than Protestant, Catholic or Jewish students who drink. The "forbidden fruit" phenomenon is demonstrable and dangerous.

It is culture, not alcohol, Mr. Hanson urges, that is the source of drinking problems. He urges several steps toward a healthier approach: (1) stop stigmatizing alcohol; (2) permit parents to serve alcohol to their children even in restaurants, (3) stress responsible drinking, not drinking itself, as a mark of maturity; (4) teach moderation, not just abstention, as responsible approaches; and (5) stop accepting intoxication as an excuse for otherwise intolerable behavior.

> "So why do teens smoke marijuana?
> . . . Curiosity is often the first
> reason."

CURIOSITY LEADS TEENAGERS INTO CHEMICAL DEPENDENCY

Roy DeLaMar

Many people believe that peer pressure is the reason teenagers begin drinking, smoking, and using drugs. In the following viewpoint, Roy DeLaMar, writing for *Family Circle* magazine, interviews teenagers and discovers that curiosity, not peer pressure, is often the reason teenagers start using mind-altering chemicals. According to the experts cited by DeLaMar, teenagers often continue to use drugs in order to cope with social and academic pressures, emotional pain, and other difficulties that adolescents frequently experience.

As you read, consider the following questions:

1. What percentage of teenagers smoke marijuana, according to the author?
2. What is the main reason teenagers drink, according to DeLaMar?
3. What advice does the author give parents who are concerned about their teenagers' becoming chemically dependent?

Excerpted from "Why 'Just Say No' Hasn't Worked: The Truth About Teens and Drugs," *Family Circle*, March 12, 1996. Reprinted with permission of *Family Circle* magazine. Copyright ©1996 by Gruner + Jahr USA Publishing.

Sixteen-year-old Cheryl Petyo is like most teenagers. She hangs out with her friends, deals with boy problems, and sometimes she keeps secrets from her parents. "I used to smoke pot," Cheryl admits. "But I only did it a couple of times. I just wanted to know what it was like."

Cheryl and her friends would get high after school, but she was careful to let the buzz wear off before heading home. "I was afraid of getting in trouble," says Cheryl, who lives in Jackson, New Jersey, with her parents and younger brother.

For a year Cheryl kept her secret well hidden. But a few months ago she gathered her courage and confessed to her mom that she had tried marijuana. "I felt deceived," admits Cheryl's mother, Glory. "It was a very rebellious period for Cheryl," she recalls. "But I never saw any sign of substance abuse."

After years of declining popularity, pot use among teens is on a serious upswing. According to the 1995 Monitoring the Future Study, an annual survey of 50,000 students conducted by the University of Michigan Institute for Social Research, marijuana use has more than doubled among eighth graders (up to 16 percent) over the previous few years. Twenty-nine percent of high school sophomores and 35 percent of seniors smoke pot. Teens are also drinking alcohol and smoking cigarettes in alarming numbers. "It's not right that marijuana is often glorified as cool," says Donna E. Shalala, U.S. Secretary of Health and Human Services. "Whether it's from TV or music, young people are receiving too many mixed messages about marijuana."

THE PEER PRESSURE MYTH

Teens who get high and those who don't agree that peer pressure has little to do with it. "My saying no now is fine with my friends," says Cheryl. "Nobody tries to force me." Experts concur that although peer pressure may be a factor, it is possible that adults have relied too heavily on it as the main reason why kids try drugs. "It's almost a cop-out," says Doug Hall, vice president of the Parents' Resource Institute for Drug Education in Atlanta. "The fact is, the largest teen peer group doesn't use drugs. Kids probably think their friends are using more than they actually are."

Fifteen-year-old Allison agrees. "I'd always wanted to try it," she says. "So I just went up to someone who dealt." Her friends played no part in it. "I like to do what I like to do," says Allison, who lives in Pennsylvania. "Peer pressure is something in textbooks.

"The third time I smoked pot, though, it wasn't the best experience. My friend told me it was laced with PCP," adds Allison. It did little to deter her, however. In fact, she doesn't consider marijuana a health risk at all.

"Teens think, 'This stuff can't hurt me,'" explains Kelly Johnson, M.D., a psychiatrist at Rush North Shore Hospital in Chicago. But it can. The pot kids smoke today is much more potent than the pot of a generation ago. In the 1960's, when marijuana first became popular, its THC (delta-9-tetrahydrocannabinol—the key mood-altering substance in pot) level was around 0.2 percent. Today's pot contains THC levels as high as 5 percent, making it 25 times stronger.

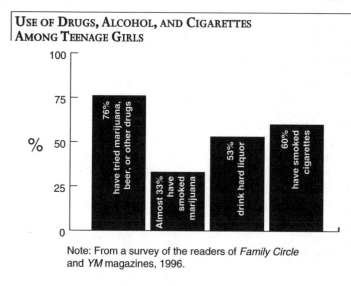

USE OF DRUGS, ALCOHOL, AND CIGARETTES AMONG TEENAGE GIRLS

- 76% have tried marijuana, beer, or other drugs
- Almost 33% have smoked marijuana
- 53% drink hard liquor
- 60% have smoked cigarettes

Note: From a survey of the readers of *Family Circle* and *YM* magazines, 1996.

Family Circle, March 12, 1996.

So why do teens smoke marijuana? Experts say curiosity is often the first reason. "Once they try it, they realize it can make them feel good," says Jeri Goodman, M.S.W., director of youth drug/alcohol prevention programs with the Single Parent Resource Center in New York. "If a teen's life isn't going the way he wants, he may keep using pot to get that 'good' feeling."

"Some kids do turn to drugs to avoid pressure, numb pain or handle depression," adds M. Duncan Stanton, Ph.D., a professor of psychiatry and psychology at the University of Rochester Medical Center in New York.

Jason, a bright 18-year-old from Glencoe, Illinois, who attends a high school that is renowned for academic excellence, claims smoking pot helps him relieve stress. "There's a real high-pressure, competitive atmosphere at my school," says Jason. "Pot helps me get 'unlearned.' It's like a little vacation from reality."....

BINGE DRINKING IS ON THE RISE

Seventeen-year-old Jennifer Dandrow doesn't drink. The Chepachet, Rhode Island, teenager's reason for staying sober is as simple as it is startling. "My grandmother was killed by a 17-year-old driver who decided to get drunk on a Tuesday afternoon," she says. Unfortunately, many teens don't follow Jennifer's example. Seventy-one percent of high school sophomores and 80 percent of seniors drink, according to the Michigan study. What's more, 30 percent of the seniors admit to binge drinking—downing more than five alcoholic beverages in a row.

With every drink, these teens put their futures—and their lives—at risk. According to the National Bureau of Economic Research in Massachusetts, students who drink alcohol are less likely to graduate from high school than their peers who don't. And about 22 percent of fatally injured 15- to 20-year-old drivers in 1994 were intoxicated.

As with marijuana use, many teens drink as an escape, but the majority simply think it's cool. "Alcohol is around my school more than weed," says Cheryl Petyo. "People still think of pot as a drug, but not alcohol." She admits that she occasionally drinks at parties or with friends. "There's usually beer, because it's easy to get," explains Cheryl....

HOW PARENTS CAN HELP

"Parents need to realize that sometimes teenagers are going to experiment in ways adults don't want them to," says Dr. Johnson, pragmatically. "But if you come down too hard on a kid, it might actually further his desire to rebel." Instead of pouncing on your teenager or trying to monitor and control his every move, experts advise talking to your child about the long-term health, legal and emotional consequences of substance use.

"It is important to confront your child if you suspect he is using, but you also need to look at why he is getting involved with drugs," advises Goodman, "Ask yourself, 'Is there something going on in my child's life that has caused drugs to become an outlet?' In our programs we teach coping skills. We want to help kids avoid using drugs to feel good or to escape. But we also need to give them other ways to handle their problems."

She suggests that you help your teen build her own extensive support systems. That way, when there is a problem, it isn't just the child and the parents. Encourage your children to establish solid relationships with other adults—relatives, teachers, athletic coaches, counselors, clergy. "Sometimes kids need alternative sources for help, other adults they trust and respect, especially in situations where they might feel uneasy coming to their parents," she says. Try not to feel threatened if your child does go outside the family for support, cautions Goodman.

If you work hard to develop openness and trust with your teenager, however, chances are she'll turn to you. Glory Petyo always hoped her children would feel able to confide in her, but Cheryl says sometimes it's not that easy. "Most kids probably aren't comfortable going to their parents because they're afraid of getting in trouble. I know I was scared when I finally told my mom that I'd smoked pot." But, she did. Now Cheryl and Glory are building a stronger, more trusting relationship.

"Glamourizing of drugs by the entertainment industry . . . has contributed to a new surge in the illegal drug consumption."

THE MEDIA'S GLAMORIZATION OF DRUG AND ALCOHOL USE CONTRIBUTES TO CHEMICAL DEPENDENCY

Mindszenty Report

Violent themes in music, movies, and television are often blamed for the high level of violence in the United States. In the following viewpoint, the editors of the Mindszenty Report contend that the media are also responsible for the increased use of drugs and alcohol by young people. MTV and other media sources often portray those who abuse drugs and alcohol in a positive light, the editors argue, thereby encouraging young people to emulate their self-destructive behavior. The Mindszenty Report is a monthly publication of conservative Catholic social and political commentary.

As you read, consider the following questions:
1. What examples do the editors give of music groups' inspiring drug abuse?
2. In what way was Kurt Cobain's death improperly reported, according to the editors?
3. What television series do the editors find particularly troubling?

"Drugs, Kids, and Culture," Mindszenty Report, January 1995. Reprinted by permission of The Cardinal Mindszenty Foundation, St. Louis, Mo.

G lamourizing of drugs by the entertainment industry, says a study conducted by the University of Michigan's Institute for Social Research, has contributed to a new surge in the illegal drug consumption by teenagers as young as 13 and 14. While smoking marijuana is the prime drug-of-choice of the young— the report points out—students from grades 8 and up are also using more cocaine, crack, heroin, hallucinogenics and stimulants. Fewer young people than ever are even *concerned* about the risks of drug use, it notes.

The Michigan Institute has been tracking teenage drug use since 1975 and annually surveys nearly 50,000 students from 420 public and private schools nationwide. Its director Dr. Lloyd D. Johnston lists various factors, such as peer pressure and relaxation of efforts by major anti-drug organizations, for the increase of teen drug use, but he emphasizes the "constant reminders in music and films that using drugs is acceptable."

But guess who the *New York Times* picked to say the Michigan Institute study was all wrong? *Not us*, the *Times* quotes Carole Robinson, senior vice-president at MTV (cable network television's 24-hour rock video channel). "While she could not speak for the industry," noted the *Times*, Ms. Robinson was certain "the music video network had 'very strict standards' and that its guidelines called for programming that did not 'promote, glamourize, or show as socially acceptable the use of illegal drugs or the abuse of legal drugs.'"

A SHOWCASE FOR DRUGS

Literally, this may be so, but in reality MTV serves as a showcase for rock and rap music groups—idolized by millions of teenagers—who do drugs. A few examples:

• A rock group called Jesus Jones, fashioning its career over MTV with only limited success, finally got celebrity notice by producing a rock video manipulating TV news footage of former president George Bush who appears to be telling Americans to take drugs.

• MTV-featured rock groups, like The Lemonheads, don't actually promote drugs on MTV, but their young fans know by reading the popular music trade magazines who they are. "I think the way the government handles drugs in this country is really hypocritical," Evan Dando of The Lemonheads tells *Rolling Stone* (11/17/94). "It's a natural impulse to want to try them . . . why deny this?" he adds.

• Another group called Negativland links its song "Christianity Is Stupid" to a drugged Minnesota teen's ax murder of his parents. Thereafter, the *New York Times* begins covering the band's appearances more extensively.

• Green Day, a group (Tre, Billie Joe and Mike) all in their early 20's, make "music for people with raging hormones and short attention spans," quips *Time* (6/27/94). Nonetheless, the magazine declares their album the "best rock release of the year" citing lyrics to a number called "Burnout" that begins: "I don't know you/But I think I hate you. . . ." On the same page *Time* raves over 43-year-old punk singer Chrissie Hynde of The Pretenders whose song "Night in My Veins" supposedly isn't about drugs but "celebrates quickie sex" with Hynde—the mother of two daughters age 11 and 9—bellowing: "Bring on the revolution/I want to die for something. . . ." Noted by *Time*: two of her charter bandmates "died of drug overdoses."

• Mega-popular grunge group Pearl Jam (you don't want to know what the name means) offers a song and video called "Jeremy" in which a prepubescent boy draped in an American flag blows his brains out in front of his sixth-grade classmates. MTV censors out the actual image of the boy placing the gun in his mouth.

"Cobain's Pain"

Drug overdosers and assorted rock-and-rap "outlaw" performers are the ones who make headlines—mostly favorable and blaming society, capitalism, their parents, the police, teachers or *whomever* for unhappinesses which are never clearly spelled out.

"He helped open people's eyes to our struggles," the *New York Times* (4/9/94) quoted a 20-year-old college student lamenting the death of "grunge rock" super-star Curt Cobain (heroin addict and suicide at age 27). What those "struggles" were, the *Times* didn't say, but five days later, still in a delirium of sorrow, theater critic Frank Rich pronounced: "The sound that (came) from his voice and his shrieking, feedback-choked guitar is the piercingly authentic cry of a child in torment." Instead of properly noting the unnecessary and tragic death of a wealthy young entertainer hooked on heroin, the media cast Cobain as a youth hero. The *Times* headlined his death "hesitant poet of grunge rock" on page one of April 9, 1994, right next to a photo of the opening of the magnificently restored Sistine Chapel in Rome.

Not only that, Cobain's photo appeared on the covers of all the major news magazines the following week, as well as most of the entertainment publications targeted at young people—all lamenting "Cobain's Pain" as symbolic of America's youth. On April 11—two days after his page-one obituary—the *Times* ran an old picture of Cobain "taping an MTV show," noting "a song called 'I Hate Myself and Want to Die' was left off 1994's In Utero album (but) appeared on 'The Beavis and Butt-Head Experience.'" (*At the 1992 MTV Video Music Awards he sang a drug song, "Lithium."*)

More on Beavis and Butt-Head later, but the furor of Cobain's group, Nirvana, and their controversial In Utero album demonstrates how young people are preyed upon by the entertainment industry. For six months giant chain stores such as Wal-Mart, Target and K-Mart would not stock the album which featured a song entitled "Rape Me" and a cover showing fetuses strewn on a field of innards.

THE GLORIFICATION OF ALCOHOL

"Absolut Magic" proclaims a print ad for a popular vodka. "Paradise found," headlines another. "Fairy tales can come true" says a third. All these ads illustrate the major premise of alcohol advertising's mythology: Alcohol is magic, a magic carpet that can take you away. It can make you successful, sophisticated, sexy. Without it, your life would be dull, mediocre and ordinary. . . . We are surrounded by the message that alcohol is fun, sexy, desirable and harmless. We get this message many times a day. We get it from the ads and, far more insidiously, we get it from the media, which depend upon alcohol advertising for a large share of their profits. Thanks to this connection, alcohol use tends to be glorified throughout the media and alcohol-related problems are routinely dismissed.

Jean Kilbourne, *Media & Values*, Spring/Summer 1991.

"We wanted to find a way of getting in there so the kids could buy the record," Geffen Records' sales executive Ray Farrell told *Entertainment Weekly* (4/8/94), because these stores are responsible for one-fourth of all record sales in the U.S. The solution: our "hesitant poet of grunge rock" retaped the song as "Waif Me" and the cover was changed displaying a plastic see-through angel with feathery wings.

While the metamorphosis didn't fool Cobain's young fans, the inclusion of a song called "Frances Farmer Will Have Her Revenge" was way over their heads. Farmer was a 1930's movie star who fronted for Hollywood's Communists and later died in an insane asylum. Cobain and his wife, rocker Courtney Love, named their daughter after her. For a short while the child was taken away by authorities after Love admitted to *Vanity Fair* magazine that she had used heroin well into her pregnancy.

With Cobain's death, Love and her band called Hole were

widely covered by the youth entertainment publications, including the news that the group's bassist Kristen Pfaff died of a heroin overdose.

TUPAC'S HISTORY OF CRIME

Yet another teen hero made the front-page of the *New York Times* (12/1/94), rap singer Tupac Shakur, described as "a heart-throb and rough-hewn idol to millions of young people who buy his records and flock to his movies. . . ."

Son of a Black Panther mom accused of conspiring to bomb department stores and police stations, Afeni Shakur named her son after the Marxist Tupac Amaru guerrillas of Uruguay. As a youngster, nonetheless, Tupac attended the prestigious Baltimore High School of Performing Arts where he studied acting and ballet. It was, however, his "lascivious rap tunes," the *Times* said, that brought him fame and fortune. His solo album "2Pacalypse Now" sold 400,000 copies and featured songs about killing policemen.

As a "gangsta rap" star, Shakur was much in demand for movies and appeared not only with Michael Jackson's sister Janet in *Poetic Justice*, but in such critically acclaimed films as *Juice* and *Above the Rim*. He also made headlines: in Los Angeles accused of beating a limo driver; in Atlanta charged but later cleared on technicalities in the shooting of two police officers; in Michigan threatening a fellow rapper with a baseball bat; in New York City, sexually assaulting a black woman in his hotel suite. What prompted the page-one headline in the *Times*: "the rough-hewn idol to millions of young people" had been shot in a robbery in downtown Manhattan and $40,000 worth of jewelry he was wearing at the time stolen.

Hundreds of innocent people are mugged and brutally assaulted each year in the streets of New York City and are never mentioned in the *Times*. Countless die of drug overdoses, but don't get page-one obituaries like Kurt Cobain. Media attention—and not talent—have made such youth-idols stars and cultural icons.

The intricate ways the popular media both manipulate and are manipulated by those who know how to tap into its power is the subject of a quirky new book, *Media Virus: Hidden Agendas in the Popular Culture*, by Douglas Rushkoff (Ballantine Books). He is a young "cyperpunk" counter-culture writer who cheerfully chronicles how ideas, images, fads, fashions, lies and propaganda have become part of the culture young people are being fed today by media activists—and not just to teenagers but much younger as well.

Kids' television, Rushkoff writes in a chapter he titles "Slip It In Their Milk," has "become, perhaps, the media's best conduit for controversial" themes . . . "new kids' TV, produced and written mostly by late baby boomers and Generation X members, are testing the limits of the tube's ability to spread counterculture messages."

SUBVERSION IN CHILDREN'S TV

"I think we are destroying the minds of America, and that's been one of my lifelong ambitions," he quotes animator John Kricfalusi in an interview in *Spin*, a popular youth music and entertainment magazine. Straight from his 1972 first-ever X-rated cartoon feature, *Fritz the Cat*, CBS hired Kricfalusi to do a Saturday-morning cartoon updating the old *Mighty Mouse* program to air following the popular *Pee-Wee's Playhouse*. After an episode showing the cartoon mouse snorting cocaine the series was canceled and Kricfalusi moved on to the Nickelodeon cable channel, owned by MTV, and a kiddies show called *Ren & Stimpy* featuring a third-world emaciated Mexican Chihuahua and a fat, dim-witted American cat.

Such "media activists" are able to use even mainstream TV to "change the way we view reality and thus reality itself," Rushkoff points out. He explains breezily:

> Mainstream media subversion is accomplished through careful and clever packaging. Commercial television activism means hiding subversive agendas in palatable candy shells. Most of us do not suspect that children's programs like "Pee-Wee's Playhouse" or "The Ren and Stimpy Show" comment on gay life styles or that "The Simpsons" and "Liquid Television" express a psychedelic world view. Children's television and MTV, in fact, are the easiest places to launch counter-culture missiles."

Here are a few other eye-opening quotes from Rushkoff's surprisingly frank exposé of media subversion and youth:

> • At first the principal theme espoused by MTV was rebellion for rebellion's sake. MTV meant watching stuff on TV that your parents couldn't understand or wouldn't approve of if they could. The choice to watch MTV was a statement of self-expression for the young viewer. . . .

> MTV's success . . . led the network into the political arena, where, for many of its viewers, it served as the only source of information. While the network strove for impartiality, MTV did endorse participation in politics and made issues like the environment, sex, and presidential elections "cool" for teenagers to care about. . . . MTV reporters almost invariably consult rock

musicians about their views on issues—rappers were interviewed about the L.A. riots . . . Axl Rose on censorship. . . .

• *The Simpsons* marks another evolutionary leap in the development of kids' TV. . . . Creator Matt Groening has long understood the way to mask his counter-culture agenda. "I find you can get away with all sorts of unusual ideas if you present them with a smile on your face.". . . The theme of *The Simpsons* is nihilism. There's nothing to believe in anymore once you assume that organized structures and institutions are out to get you . . . this is the American media family turned on its head. . . . Currently in the mainstream media, it is only kids' TV that has a sufficiently innocuous appearance to permit its irreverence. The audience interested in its subversive attitudes is not large enough to keep the show in business, but the millions of kids who tune in every week to watch Bart are. A popular animated children's show is the perfect virus. It spreads for one reason, then releases potent (messages) that do not seem evident on the surface.

• MTV's *Beavis and Butt-Head* are now internationally famous for the afternoons they spend together watching MTV . . . but most adults do not understand the instructional agenda of *Beavis and Butt-Head*. They only see two ugly adolescents destroying things and millions of teenagers enjoying the destruction. . . .

A MEDIA WAR AGAINST YOUTH

With so much media sedition aimed at young people, is it any wonder that increased use of drugs—as well as violence, sexual promiscuity and disinterest in education—increases from year to year?

We are entering the last years of the 20th century, writes UCLA Professor James Q. Wilson in the scholarly *Manhattan Institute's City Journal*, "with every reason to rejoice and little inclination to do so, despite widespread prosperity, a generally healthy economy, the absence of any immediate foreign threat, and extraordinary progress in civil rights, personal health and school enrollment . . . *despite all this and more, we feel that there is something profoundly wrong with our society.*"

Why, he asks? He says that one prime reason is "the cultural perspective," as follows: "Child rearing and family life as traditionally understood can no longer compete with or bring under prudent control a culture of radical self-indulgence and oppositional defiance, fostered by drugs, television, video games, street gangs and predatory sexuality."

To deal with this cultural assault on America's youth will require the concerted action of religious and cultural leaders, parents and young people working together to expose the maliciousness of the attackers.

In another time and place—at the end of WWII—Joseph Cardinal Mindszenty agonized over "sad young people" he said who "want to strike up dance music in such a tragic hour . . . in the midst of the blood and the ruins, the poverty and tears, these children are making merry. Indeed they know not what they do." (*Memoirs*, p. 259)

In the fast approaching 21st century, those thoughts might well be remembered as the media's war escalates against our youth.

PERIODICAL BIBLIOGRAPHY

The following articles have been selected to supplement the diverse views presented in this chapter. Addresses are provided for periodicals not indexed in the *Readers' Guide to Periodical Literature*, the *Alternative Press Index*, the *Social Sciences Index*, or the *Index to Legal Periodicals and Books*.

Jonathan Beaty	"Do Humans Need to Get High?" *Time*, August 21, 1989.
Susan Gilbert	"Why Some Light Drinkers at Age Twenty May Still Be on Track to Alcoholism," *New York Times*, March 13, 1996.
Daniel Goleman	"Study Ties Genes to Alcoholism in Women," *New York Times*, October 14, 1992.
Wayne Hearn	"Co-dependents," *American Medical News*, May 23–30, 1994. Available from 515 N. State St., Chicago, IL 60610.
Art Levine	"America's Addiction to Addictions," *U.S. News & World Report*, February 5, 1990.
Robert M. Morse and Daniel K. Flavin	"The Definition of Alcoholism," *JAMA*, August 26, 1992.
Stanton Peele	"Control Yourself," *Reason*, February 1990.
Andrew Purvis	"DNA and the Desire to Drink," *Time*, April 30, 1990.
David Rieff	"Victims All? Recovery, Co-dependency, and the Art of Blaming Somebody Else," *Harper's Magazine*, October 1991.
Jeffrey A. Schaler	"Drugs and Free Will," *Society*, September/October 1991.
Marc A. Schuckit	"Is There a Link Between Substance Use Disorders and Eating Disorders?" *Drug Abuse & Alcoholism Newsletter*, December 1995. Available from Vista Hill Foundation, 2355 Northside Dr., 3rd Fl., San Diego, CA 92108.
Marc A. Schuckit	"Is There a Relationship Between Hyperactivity in Childhood and the Risk for Alcoholism?" *Drug Abuse & Alcoholism Newsletter*, October 1995.
Linda Troiano	"Addicted States of America," *American Health*, September 1990.

CHAPTER 3

WHAT TREATMENTS ARE EFFECTIVE FOR CHEMICAL DEPENDENCY?

CHAPTER PREFACE

Carolyn Watson was a crack cocaine addict who stole and worked as a prostitute to pay for her habit. New York City child welfare officials took her two children from her because of her inability to care for them. She lived on the streets.

But after seven months in a Bronx treatment center, Watson was drug-free and able to take care of her children once again. She became an "A" student in college and worked toward her bachelor's degree in social work. She became an active, involved parent.

The treatment program Watson entered included therapy, parenting classes, and child care. It worked for Watson. But it does not work for most addicts: Only about one out of seven who enter the program graduate. In addition, although treatment can work miracles in the lives of individual addicts, the majority of addicts do not conquer their habit in one course of treatment. Watson needed three tries at treatment before succeeding.

The types of treatment available for chemical addiction vary greatly, depending upon the type of addiction, the financial and social resources of the addict, the severity of the addiction, and other factors. Treatment experts are realizing that treatment needs to be individualized to be successful—that what works for one addict may not work for another. For example, Alcoholics Anonymous (AA) is considered by many to be the most effective treatment program for alcoholism. However, according to Joann Ellison Rodgers of the Johns Hopkins School of Hygiene and Public Health, several studies have found that "AA simply doesn't work for a lot of people."

The following chapter describes various types of treatment for alcoholics and drug addicts. It also explores the question of why addiction is so difficult to overcome and what factors enable some people to combat addiction while others are unable to break its grip.

| "Acupuncture-based programs offer healing and thus hope to addicts and to their loved ones."

ACUPUNCTURE CAN HELP TREAT CHEMICAL DEPENDENCY

Ellinor R. Mitchell

Acupuncture is an ancient Chinese method of healing in which needles are inserted into the patient's skin at specific points on the body in an attempt to cure disease or relieve pain. In the following viewpoint, Ellinor R. Mitchell argues that acupuncture is an effective way of helping people combat chemical dependency and should be seriously considered as a low-cost, humane form of treatment for addiction. Mitchell is a New York–based writer and community activist and the author of two books on acupuncture, including *Fighting Drug Abuse with Acupuncture: The Treatment That Works*, from which this viewpoint is excerpted.

As you read, consider the following questions:

1. What statistics does the author cite to support her contentions that chemical dependency imposes a huge burden on society?
2. How is acupuncture performed, as described by Mitchell?
3. Why does Mitchell believe acupuncture treatment is "a health-care bargain"?

We foot the bill for substance abuse—whether we allocate tax dollars to healing, which in the process of change offers hope, or to building more prisons which simply warehouse addicts until they are released to pursue the same old life and do not change drug-seeking behavior.

The misery shared by millions of addicts, their families and their friends cannot be quantified, only experienced or observed. Addiction's cost to society, however, *can* be calculated: The price for substance abuse—the term coined years ago to describe addiction to both illegal and legal drugs—is $237.5 billion per year, according to an estimate published by the Robert Wood Johnson Foundation (*Substance Abuse: The Nation's Number One Health Problem*).

The Johnson Foundation report assigns $66.9 billion of the annual $237.5 billion price tag to drug abuse, $98.6 billion to alcohol abuse and $72 billion to smoking. The report estimates that substance-abuse-related expenses—costs which would not be incurred were it not for addiction's daunting prevalence—equal $1,000 per year taken from every man, woman and child in this country. . . .

Treatment for illegal drug use and alcoholism has existed for decades, but still it is neither plentiful nor always attractive to clients. The prevailing national estimate is that conventional treatment—therapeutic communities and hospital inpatient or outpatient services, among other settings—serves one addict in four.

Between 1985 and 1995, $14 billion was spent on high-tech, high-cost approaches to cutting the drug supply, to no effect. Low-tech but definitely high-cost imprisonment—for the most part, with very little treatment available—has not deterred drug use and drug dealing.

An Alternative

But there does exist an innovative, low-cost, effective means of treating addiction to illegal drugs and to alcohol, the preeminent legal drug. This approach, using acupuncture, has a twenty-year track record and is gaining acceptance by agencies and institutions deeply frustrated by past failure. Three hundred health facilities in twenty states now provide drug-abuse treatment that uses acupuncture according to a therapeutic design originating at Lincoln Hospital in New York. Nine other countries have programs based on this method, which among other things uses ear-acupuncture, chamomile-based herbal tea and regular urine testing.

For too long, those who insist drug addiction is purely a crime to be punished have contended with those who see it as a disease to be treated. The experience of rehabilitating addicts by treating addiction as a disease rather than a crime discredits proposals to pour billions of dollars into the prison industry to punish people rather than help them recover. Acupuncture-based treatment works. Clinic by clinic it is supplanting the vindictive attitude of jail-builders and of those who purport to wage a "war" on drugs.

Since 1989 a court in Dade County, Florida, has demonstrated the economic common sense and compassion of a therapeutic approach to coping with drug addicts arrested for nonviolent offenses. Of 6,000 people accepted into the program since it began, 3,480 have completed it; 1,200 are currently enrolled [as of 1995]. Nationally, 60 percent of people arrested on drug charges are rearrested. But the rearrest rate for graduates of Dade County's drug court is under 40 percent.

By late 1994, of the more than 6,000 who had entered the Miami program, 72 percent stayed in treatment; 28 percent either dropped out or were rearrested and dismissed from the program. Dade's Diversion and Treatment Program costs out at $500 to $750 per participant per year—less than 4 percent of the annual cost per inmate for imprisonment in Florida.

Miami's program is a leading example of acupuncture's practical power to keep nonviolent defendants in treatment and out of jail. The drug court's philosophy is finding increasing acceptance in the criminal justice system. By late 1993, eight other Florida counties—Broward, Escambia, Hillsborough, Lee, Leon, Monroe, Palm Beach, and Pinellas—had adopted the Dade County model. Nationwide, drug courts have been formed in Mobile, Alabama; Little Rock, Arkansas; St. Joseph, Michigan; Kansas City, Missouri; Las Vegas, Nevada; Portland, Oregon; and Austin and Beaumont, Texas. Acupuncture is integral to all these court-linked treatment programs.

INTEREST IN ACUPUNCTURE IS GROWING

The First National Drug Court Conference, held in Miami in December 1993, was funded by the National Institute of Justice and planned as a small working group to discuss drug court issues. This event attracted more than 400 people from all over the United States. Judges, defense lawyers, prosecutors and other members of the criminal justice community, as well as drug-treatment providers, were addressed by U.S. Attorney General Janet Reno. She noted the drug court movement's astonishing growth. Attendees observed Miami's drug court, and exchanged information about initiating and conducting similar venues— courts intimately involved in treatment of drug offenders.

CONTROLLING ADDICTS' HOSTILITIES

Acupuncture not only controls withdrawal symptoms and craving, but it also reduces fears and hostilities that usually disturb drug abuse treatment settings. Acupuncture has a balancing effect on the autonomic and neurotransmitter systems as well as an apparently rejuvenating effect.

Michael O. Smith, testimony before the U.S. House of Representatives, July 25, 1989.

Acupuncture-based addiction treatment, codified and disseminated by the National Acupuncture Detoxification Association (NADA), takes place in many different settings. Among them are community health clinics, court-affiliated programs in which defendants may choose treatment instead of incarceration, halfway houses, jails, prisons and a variety of other criminal justice facilities. Private mental health clinics employ the treatment as do methadone maintenance programs, municipal hospitals, Native American chemical-dependency clinics and counseling centers both urban and rural. Clients of acupuncture-based programs include adults and infants, people headed for jail and those already incarcerated, those whose chief distinguishing problem is addiction, and those for whom addiction is just one health disorder among many, including AIDS.

PART OF A COMPREHENSIVE TREATMENT PROGRAM

A typical effective and comprehensive yet inexpensive rehabilitation program combines acupuncture with group work such as 12-Step meetings and individual counseling. Programs of this type are being used successfully in the United States from New York's South Bronx to Indian reservations, and abroad from the slums of London through Western Europe and Hungary to Katmandu.

In South Dakota, acupuncture-based programs treat Native American alcoholics. A New York City clinic is helping to break the multigenerational cycle of child abuse in a program that combines acupuncture with comprehensive treatment of drug-using parents. Prisoners in Minnesota receive acupuncture for substance abuse problems. An acupuncture-based general clinic in Oregon also offers substance abuse treatment to its clients, some of whom are HIV-positive.

Acupuncture-based programs offer healing and thus hope to addicts and to their loved ones, who have said all too often, "He's finally getting it together, trying a new program," or, "This time she's been clean for a month; maybe she'll make it." Some people have, too often, been summoned to a hospital only to watch someone die. Acupuncture-based treatment is very good news for our drug-ridden society.

DRUG ABUSE IS PERVASIVE

Experts on the drug plague say that treatment works. But as anyone who cares about an addicted person knows, it is often a struggle to get chemically dependent people into treatment and to retain them in a process that goes beyond detoxification to recovery and maintenance of recovery, and thereby changes their lives.

Some people enter addiction treatment voluntarily. Many are prodded by criminal justice and social service agencies to enroll in treatment programs as a condition of probation—a period of supervision in lieu of incarceration—or of parole—time after release from prison that completes the term of a sentence. For others, it is a condition for regaining child custody.

Industrial and office workers are candidates for cure, as are corporate CEOs. Addiction is an equal opportunity affliction. While the media repeatedly emphasize the problem of drugs in the black community—almost to the point of racist stereotyping—the fact is that addiction to drugs, both legal and illegal, pervades our whole society. . . .

A GATEWAY TO RECOVERY

Entering treatment is crucial. However, addicted people tend to drop out of treatment when they feel better, or when short-term goals are achieved. But recovery from addiction is long-term, which is why some groups, like Alcoholics Anonymous, regard it as a lifelong process.

Acupuncture detoxification is a gateway to recovery. Thousands of documented clinical cases show that drug-addicted patients like the effects of acupuncture. They say it calms the spirit, reduces cravings and alleviates tension, anxiety and dread. An acupuncture drug-treatment clinic, where many people sit in a treatment room with needles in their ears, is a tranquil place—most clients appear to be meditating. The atmosphere provides the luxury of peacefulness, a quality lacking in the life of anyone gripped by addiction.

Wherever it is practiced, the acupuncture-detoxification procedure is basically the same. You sit in a room with other clients and, like them, have three to five very fine acupuncture needles inserted at specific locations in the outer ear. The needles go under the skin, *not* through the ear. Any slight pain you might feel is fleeting. You've been through worse, or you wouldn't have come here. You sit and relax—yes! Relax.

What do you feel? The usual sensation is a release of tension—the insistent tension that obsessively repeats, "I need my fix," or "I gotta have a drink." Many acupuncture patients report, "It just feels like you've come home." Perhaps you will drift into meditation, or just sit watching your thoughts go by, maybe thinking about the last time you tried to kick, maybe wondering if you know the guy three chairs away. He looks familiar. . . .

About 45 minutes later, the needles are removed. You may sit for a while before going back outside into the world. Either at the time of your admission, or after treatment, you receive tea bags containing an herbal mix which is nonnarcotic but helps you relax. You may drink a cup of this anytime, but must be sure to have some at bedtime. You feel better. You return the next day.

The procedures described here are becoming standard, but clinical variations do occur, as is often the case in conventional therapies.

PREVENTING RELAPSE

Detox generally involves daily ear-acupuncture treatments. During this period you give a urine sample before each treatment. The sample is computer-analyzed: day by day you see a printout. When you have drugs in your system, the computer reports this on paper. Slipping isn't good, but everybody in the clinic knows it happens. When your printout shows ten consecutive clean urines, the next stage of the process begins: you continue to give urines and receive ear-acupuncture, while also participating in Narcotics Anonymous (NA) or Alcoholics Anonymous (AA), generally referred to as 12-Step groups.

Acupuncture-based programs *attract* addicted people by accepting walk-in clients as well as those referred by criminal justice or social service agencies, and by keeping intake paperwork to a minimum. They *retain* clients because acupuncture supports the hard work of becoming clean and sober, and of going on to engage in other elements of comprehensive treatment, including 12-Step work, prenatal care for pregnant addicts, group and individual counseling, men's groups, women's groups, educational and vocational placement, and other social services. Since it can be applied as needed to support a patient's recovery, acupuncture is the finest kind of insurance policy for chemically dependent people whose illness is characterized by relapse.

Acupuncture-based addiction treatment is a health-care bargain. It is a bargain for clients, many of whom have custody of children, go to school, and have jobs. (In 1990 William Bennett, federal "drug czar," said that "seventy percent of the regular drug users in the United States hold full-time jobs.") Outpatient treatment avoids radical disruption of whatever degree of normalcy clients have been able to maintain despite their illness. Fees are generally on a sliding scale, pegged to income, with Medicaid payment usually accepted. Such programs are cost-effective to city, county and state institutions because outpatient acupuncture treatment is inexpensive. Hospitalization can often be avoided, or if not avoided, curtailed. Treatment of pregnant cocaine users means more babies carried to term and of good birth-weight, thus not requiring intensive-care hospitalization.

"The biofeedback trainees achieved an unprecedented 80 percent abstinence rate."

BIOFEEDBACK CAN HELP TREAT CHEMICAL DEPENDENCY

Jim Robbins

Biofeedback is a medical therapy in which patients can treat themselves by learning to control their own brain waves. In the following viewpoint, Jim Robbins explains how biofeedback works to help reduce the cravings caused by alcoholism and drug abuse. Robbins, a freelance writer in Helena, Montana, argues that biofeedback could become a commonly used, effective treatment for chemical dependency.

As you read, consider the following questions:
1. How does biofeedback work, according to Robbins?
2. What are the four types of brain waves cited by the author?
3. What are some theories as to why biofeedback is an effective treatment for chemical dependency, according to Robbins?

Abridged from "Wired for Miracles" by Jim Robbins, New Age Journal, March/April 1996. Reprinted by permission of New Age Journal, 42 Pleasant St., Watertown, MA 02172; $24/year. For subscriptions, call (815) 734-5808.

When Mary Obringer and her husband adopted a five-month-old South Korean baby in May of 1987, she knew immediately that something was wrong. "He developed slowly," Obringer says of the infant, whom they named Max. "He had speech disabilities, motor skill problems, social problems. He was hyperactive and had trouble concentrating." As a toddler, Max couldn't be in a large group of people without getting violent—hitting, kicking, and screaming. By the time he started kindergarten, in Jackson, Wyoming, "It was clear right away he wasn't going to be able to stay." Even after doctors diagnosed the boy with attention deficit disorder (ADD) and put him on the drug Ritalin, Max's condition still required that he be in a special-education classroom. The family's frustration level was reaching a peaking point. And then they met psychologist Michael Enright.

WORKING WONDERS

Enright, a member of the oversight board of the American Psychological Association, told Obringer he knew of a treatment that might help her son. The treatment was EEG biofeedback—a promising new approach that teaches patients to consciously recognize and control their own brain-wave patterns.

Obringer was more than willing to give it a try. Twice a week for the next six months, she brought Max to his thirty-minute treatments in Enright's small, darkened EEG room at the Jackson hospital. At the start of each session, Enright would dab globs of conducting paste on Max's scalp and attach two electrodes to amplify his brain waves, which were displayed on a computer screen. A second machine was set up to run a variation of the popular video game Pac-Man.

Instead of using buttons or a joystick, however, Max would play this game with his brain waves alone. Whenever he generated certain patterns associated with alert concentration, the little yellow monster would gobble his way around a maze to reward him. And the more he played, the better his technique became: As the weeks went on, Max became something of a pro at generating those focused brain waves.

Today, Obringer believes that EEG feedback has worked wonders for her son. "We started seeing immediate results," she recalls. "Within a couple of weeks he could sit in a chair and not fidget." The violent outbursts stopped, too—"no kicking, no hitting, no fighting," his mother says with relief. And though he still needs to take Ritalin, Max has begun to spend part of every day in a regular classroom. "He's like every other kid," she concludes, gratefully.

Max is one of a growing number of people turning to EEG biofeedback—a cutting-edge, if controversial, treatment used to relieve a host of health complaints, both mental and physical. Though some forms of EEG biofeedback have been around since the 1970s, today researchers and practitioners are directing the technique toward more than alleviating anxiety and stress. Problems as diverse as closed-head injury, alcoholism, and learning disabilities are being addressed by teaching people to consciously change the rhythms in their own brain.

"The field is just exploding," says Joel Lubar, a professor of psychology at the University of Tennessee and incoming president of the Association for Applied Psychophysiology and Biofeedback (AAPB), the professional association that represents the biofeedback field. Indeed, the Association has seen the number of EEG specialists in its membership grow from a handful a decade ago to a full 500 of its 2,300 members today. Among them are psychologists, nurses, physicians, and educational specialists variously affiliated with hospitals, clinics, university research centers, and doctors' offices. All of them practice a treatment that would seem the ultimate in self-healing: training the brain to fix its own disorders.

REPROGRAMMING THE BRAIN

By broad definition, the term *biofeedback* refers to the process in which subtle information on how a person's body and brain are operating is amplified and shown back to that person. Simple devices measuring muscle tension and body temperature, for example, help people learn to regulate their blood pressure, temperature, and other physical and mental processes not typically under their conscious control. Many forms of biofeedback are now well established as treatments for stress-related conditions such as migraine headaches and chronic pain. Today these types of biofeedback are not only practiced at such bastions of mainstream medicine as the Mayo Clinic, but are increasingly being paid for by insurance companies as well.

The branch of the field known as EEG biofeedback has remained more controversial. Indeed, only in the last few years has this approach attracted widespread research interest or clinical use. Its premise: that many conditions—from learning disabilities to depression to panic attacks—can be helped by teaching patients how to alter their brainwave patterns.

In a typical EEG biofeedback session, electrodes are placed on the scalp to pick up brain-wave activity. ("No electricity goes into the brain," one practitioner told us reassuringly.) The brain-wave information is then fed into a computer, which translates its patterns into a user-friendly display on the screen—a game showing cars speeding along a highway, say, or small squares whose size and color can be changed. There's only one catch with these computer games: You can't use your hands. Instead, the object is to try to manipulate what happens on the screen by mind power alone.

HEARING NEW RHYTHMS

Essentially, biofeedback is a way to train the body to alter biological functions using correcting signals. One researcher compares it to learning to play the piano. At first it is difficult to hear if you are playing the correct notes. But with practice, it becomes easier to know, and easier to figure out how to correct mistakes. Biofeedback is a way to train the body to "hear" new rhythms.

Anita Bartholomew, Omni, December 1994.

While this kind of no-hands Nintendo may sound impossible, practitioners say that, through trial and error, users can actually be trained to increase and decrease their brain waves at will. "It's like learning to ride a bicycle: You learn by experimenting," says one. (EEG biofeedback therapy used to induce brain waves associated with relaxation is a simpler process: Electrodes are attached to devices that emit audible tones when the person gets into a relaxed state.) Sessions typically last from forty-five minutes to an hour, and an entire treatment program can take from ten to sixty sessions, depending on the condition being addressed.

Where other forms of biofeedback aim to teach people a skill they can call upon in specific situations—for example, learning to relax deeply to head off an impending migraine headache—EEG biofeedback may have a more enduring goal: to "retrain the brain" so it gets in the habit of producing healthy brainwave patterns on its own thereafter.

BRAIN-WAVE BASICS

To appreciate the different ways EEG biofeedback is being applied today, it helps to understand some brain-wave basics. The brain continuously produces combinations of four distinct frequencies, or speeds, of brain waves—delta, theta, alpha, and beta—and our state of consciousness depends on which of these waves is dominant. When we sleep, delta waves take over, with their slow-moving signals traveling at up to 4 cycles per second, or four hertz (Hz). Slightly faster are theta waves (4 to 8 Hz), associated with the twilight consciousness on the brink of sleep in which dreamlike mental images can surface. Above theta is alpha (8 to 12 Hz), the calm and mentally unfocused state typically connected with relaxation. In our normal waking state, when our eyes are open and focused on the world, beta waves are in charge. Within beta itself, scientists recognize a range—from low beta, a relaxed but alert state of 12 to 15 Hz, to the excited, anxious state of high beta, which can climb as high as 35 Hz.

Much of the early interest in EEG biofeedback focused on helping people learn to generate waves associated with deep relaxation: alpha and theta. Alpha-theta biofeedback was pioneered in the '70s by Elmer and Alyce Green of the Menninger Clinic in Topeka, Kansas—still a leading center for biofeedback research—and Joe Kamiya, a researcher in San Francisco. The researchers found that if biofeedback users were alerted with an audible tone when they generated sufficient alpha waves, the subjects could, in just a session or two, get into a deeply relaxed state—a state as deep as that reached by people who'd meditated for years. Today, alpha training is commonly practiced to reduce stress and anxiety, and to help manage pain.

TREATING ADDICTION

Recently, however, researchers have begun studying some surprising new applications for alpha-theta training. In one provocative, if small-scale, 1989 study, Eugene Peniston, a clinical psychologist then of Fort Lyon Veterans Affairs Medical Center in Fort Lyon, Colorado, gave ten chronic alcoholics thirty sessions of biofeedback training focused on boosting their alpha and theta waves. A second group was given conventional treatment, including participation in a twelve-step program and antidepressant medications. As part of what has since become known as the "Peniston protocol," alcoholics in the first group were coached in basic relaxation techniques, trained to boost their own alpha-theta waves, and led through visualization and imagery exercises (such as scenes in which they saw themselves refusing an offered drink). Counseling was also provided to help subjects work through any images and feelings that might surface.

At the end of a month of treatment, the biofeedback trainees achieved an unprecedented 80 percent abstinence rate, compared to 20 percent in the conventional group. What's more, when the trainees were followed up five years after treatment's end, their recovery rate remained an impressive 70 percent, having declined by only 10 percent.

What's to account for the dramatic shift? Alcoholics before treatment have trouble reaching and staying in the alpha state, where "self-soothing" neurotransmitters are produced, theorize researchers. Often they turn to alcohol as an artificial means of inducing this state of relaxation. But as biofeedback treatment progresses, and those self-soothing neurotransmitters begin to flow, the craving for a drink may be reduced.

Another possible reason for biofeedback's effectiveness is that it can help subjects stay in a theta, or *hypnogogic*, state for a sustained period of time. While people pass through theta on their way to sleep every night, they quickly move on to delta. "EEG helps people linger in theta," says Dale Walters, of Topeka, Kansas, who conducted biofeedback at the Menninger Clinic and is currency working to set up a six-week outpatient biofeedback program to treat addiction in Kansas City, Missouri. In a theta state, says Walters, childhood memories and buried emotions bubble spontaneously to the surface. With the help of a psychologist, he says, such associations can often be worked through. "Those experiences lead to unblocking of intense emotions," says Walters.

Peniston's treatment is slowly beginning to make inroads into clinical settings. In Topeka, Kansas, the Life Sciences Institute of Mind-Body Health now offers an intensive outpatient program that includes seven weeks of two-and-a-half-hour daily alpha-theta training sessions, coupled with intensive psychotherapy. According to Carol Snarr, a registered nurse and biofeedback therapist at the Institute, the program has so far treated not only alcoholics but also drug addicts, people with eating disorders, even smokers, some of whom have come across the country for treatment. "It is truly a way to integrate body, mind, emotion, and spirit," she says. Over the next few years, the Institute will be following patients' progress as part of a long-term follow-up study on Peniston's findings.

> "There is evidence that spirituality is an element in recovery from addiction."

RELIGION CAN HELP TREAT CHEMICAL DEPENDENCY

Larry Witham

While most physicians and therapists focus on medical and psychological treatments for chemical dependency, an increasing number of experts now emphasize the role religion and spirituality can play in fighting addiction. In the following viewpoint, Larry Witham presents the views of researchers who believe that by bringing joy and meaning to addicts' lives, religion can cure them of the craving for drugs. Witham is a writer for the *Washington Times* newspaper.

As you read, consider the following questions:

1. According to Roy Matthews, cited by the author, how does spiritual activity affect the brain?
2. What religious groups have successfully fought addiction, according to Witham?
3. What is the "Ebenezer Scrooge" effect, as explained by the author?

As medical science continues its struggle to free people of drug and alcohol addiction, a group of top clinicians is researching a novel antidote—the natural high that comes from imbibing the spirit.

The new clinical emphasis on religious solutions to addiction is being dovetailed with a standard therapeutic model that holds that drug dependency is caused by the pleasure deficit resulting when a sober life lacks stimulation or meaning for a person.

"There is evidence that spirituality is an element in recovery from addiction," said Dr. William Miller, research director for the Center on Alcoholism, Substance Abuse and Addiction at the University of New Mexico. Yet religion is ignored as a therapeutic tool because conventional researchers "don't have a clue how to measure spiritual constructs," Dr. Miller said at a national conference in April 1995 in Lansdowne, Virginia. "Simply to ignore such a major source of potential healing is to violate scientific curiosity."

The three-day meeting, "Spiritual Dimensions in Clinical Research," was described by many of the 70 participants as a major step toward moving research on "the R-word"—religion—into mainstream medical science.

A Problem with Pleasure

Summarizing research findings, several speakers characterized the substance-addicted life as lacking meaning and purpose, craving pleasure, or reaching a state of "joylessness."

"Drug abuse is not a problem with drugs, it's a problem with pleasure," said Dr. Roy Matthews, head of the Duke University Medical Center's alcoholism and addiction program. He described pleasure as a chemically driven "insatiable" drive in people.

"Pleasure is the basis of addiction, and it would seem pleasure is a solution to addiction," he said. "There is a difference in the quality of self-based pleasure and selfless pleasure, which can produce a certain mood state in you. The most pleasurable part of religion is the experience of God."

Spiritual Activity as Drug

He said that dopamine, a chemical produced in the brain, acts on neurons to create sensations of well-being and euphoria. Based on research of the brain's blood flow and alpha waves, he suggested that spiritual activity by the mind may have a similar chemical effect.

Dr. Frank Gawin, senior psychiatrist for drug-abuse research at the University of California at Los Angeles, said that cocaine withdrawal is clinically recognized as "anhedonia," or "the absence of joy and the intensification of boredom."

"Addiction is a kind of craving," he said. "It may be in [the medical study of] craving that we have a door between science and the spiritual."

The vast research done on addicted populations, Dr. Gawin said, may make it the area of medicine in which spiritual elements—which are associated with particular psychological effects—can be included in controlled scientific studies.

Source: Rex Babin. Reprinted with special permission of North America Syndicate.

Outside of clinical or population studies, he said, religious groups have proven success in breaking addictions, such as programs for opium field workers in Buddhist Thailand and Muslim Pakistan.

During Japan's methamphetamine blight in the 1950s and 1960s, Zen temples had the most effective treatment programs, he said. And the Bahamas staunched a crack cocaine epidemic in 1983–1985 mostly through church basement clinics.

A main testing ground of spiritual therapy for addiction has been Alcoholics Anonymous, which has a 12-step program that stresses putting the problem in the care of a higher power, the researchers said.

Dr. Miller cited data on how AA members who make strong commitments to the spiritual basis of the program gain sufficient "meaning in life" to displace the need for alcohol.

AA founder Bill Wilson, an alcoholic himself, started the movement after being freed from alcohol craving by a sudden religious experience one day in the 1930s in New York.

Though such euphoria would be the most difficult to subject to controlled study, new research is at least trying to identify the traits of "the quantum-change experience, in which a personality is turned upside down," Dr. Miller said.

THE "EBENEZER SCROOGE" EFFECT

Often called the "Ebenezer Scrooge" effect, it is traditionally associated with religious conversion. But Dr. Miller said that people seem to have it in a variety of ways.

He interviewed 54 persons from a larger sample who claimed such an experience and found that 57 percent had their "quantum change" during a time of distress. However, 46 percent faced nothing unusual at the time of their experience.

For the majority, the experience lasted less than 24 hours, and 96 percent said the sense of "new meaning" in life changed how they lived. "There is nothing you can do to bring it on," Dr. Miller said. "It just happens to people."

Dr. David Larson, an epidemiologist who heads the independent National Institute for Healthcare Research, said clinical journals have scores of positive correlations between religion and health, but it has been ignored or hidden because of secular bias in the research field.

"Methadone is far more likely to help heroin addicts regain control of their lives than is any other therapy."

METHADONE CAN HELP TREAT HEROIN ADDICTION

Adam Yarmolinsky and Constance M. Pechura

Methadone is a drug that prevents withdrawal symptoms in heroine addicts who quit using heroin. In the following viewpoint, Adam Yarmolinsky and Constance M. Pechura describe the benefits of government methadone treatment programs for addicts. The authors insist that these programs are effective and that they should be more readily available. Yarmolinsky is a professor of public policy at the University of Maryland, Baltimore County, in Catonsville, and chairman of the Institute of Medicine's (IOM) Committee on the Federal Regulation of Methadone Treatment. Pechura is the director of the IOM's Division of Biobehavioral Science and Mental Disorders.

As you read, consider the following questions:

1. Why are the regulations concerning the use of methadone so restrictive, in the authors' opinion?
2. What are the two basic types of methadone treatment, according to Yarmolinsky and Pechura?
3. How do the authors respond to the argument that easing regulations on methadone would result in abuse of the drug?

Heroin addiction continues to do inestimable damage not only to the lives of addicted individuals, but also to families, neighborhoods, cities, and society as a whole. The tragedy is that although we know how to treat heroin addiction, we have tied the hands of the physicians and other health care workers who are trying to help.

Methadone treatment has been widely shown during the past three decades to help heroin addicts free themselves from drug dependency, from a life of crime in support of their habit, and from increased risk of adding to the nation's AIDS population by sharing dirty needles. Indeed, methadone is far more likely to help heroin addicts regain control of their lives than is any other therapy. Tens of thousands of addicts who were a burden and often a threat to society have become productive citizens as a result of methadone treatment.

RIGID REGULATION

Yet despite methadone's effectiveness, we have created a complex web of government regulations that interferes significantly with treatment programs. At the federal level, both the Food and Drug Administration (FDA) and the Drug Enforcement Administration (DEA) have broad regulatory authority. In principle, FDA is responsible for examining the quality of the programs based on detailed mandated requirements, and DEA is responsible for monitoring compliance with security measures and record keeping requirements; in practice, both agencies routinely extend their oversight beyond these boundaries. In addition, the Department of Health and Human Services has established special standards prescribing how and under what circumstances methadone may be used to treat opiate addiction. These standards are implemented by FDA regulations, jointly with the National Institute on Drug Abuse and the Substance Abuse and Mental Health Services Administration. State governments often impose even more stringent regulations—indeed, 10 states have decided against making methadone treatment available at all— and county and city governments frequently pile on their own requirements.

These various levels of regulation cover methadone treatment down to the finest detail. For example, federal regulations rigidly set patient admission criteria, define acceptable methadone dose levels, and limit service sites, which often means that physicians cannot provide treatment in the manner that is best for an individual patient. There are also undue administrative burdens (for example, physicians are required to apply every year for a special federal license and programs are subject to multiple inspections, often by untrained and inexperienced inspectors) that reduce the effectiveness and increase the cost of treatment programs, many of which are already financially strapped. No other type of medication is so highly regulated.

Yet, according to a 1995 Institute of Medicine (IOM) study with which we were involved, there is no compelling medical reason for regulating methadone differently from all other medications approved by FDA. Our committee concluded that current policy puts too much emphasis on protecting society from the extremely limited risk that methadone might be diverted from treatment programs to the street and not enough on protecting society from the epidemics of addiction, violence, and infectious diseases that methadone can help reduce.

HELPING ADDICTS KICK THEIR HABIT

Thus, the scope of government regulation at all levels should be greatly reduced in favor of authorizing greater clinical discretion in determining appropriate medical treatment. The recent development of a new, longer-acting analog of methadone (an agent known as LAMM, which offers improved treatment but is covered by even tighter restrictions than those placed on its older relative) makes it all the more urgent that providers be unshackled from counterproductive regulations.

The benefits of such regulatory modifications would be considerable. Patients would have access to treatment programs tailored to their circumstances. Physicians would be better able to exercise their professional judgment. Treatment programs could be better integrated into mainstream medical care, which would allow patients to more easily obtain important ancillary health and social services that boost the odds that treatment will be successful. And treatment costs, which are shared by programs, patients, insurers, and taxpayers, would be cut—probably dramatically.

The overall result, if our recommendations are followed, would be that heroin addicts would receive the best treatment possible to help them kick their habit. And many more addicts could be treated. Today, only 125,000 of the estimated half-million to 1 million addicts in this country are receiving some type of methadone treatment.

TWO TYPES OF TREATMENT

Methadone is a weak-acting synthetic opiate agonist—that is, it imitates the action of an opiate, such as heroin—that does not generate the euphoria of an opiate but does reduce symptoms of opiate withdrawal. In the mid-1960s, methadone was shown to be effective in the treatment of opiate addiction, and thereafter it became widely available for this use

There are two basic types of methadone treatment: medically supervised withdrawal (called "detoxification treatment" in federal regulations) and maintenance pharmacotherapy (called "methadone maintenance" in the regulations). In withdrawal therapy, which is used for about 8 percent of the heroin addicts in treatment, methadone is administered at a steadily reduced dose over a limited period of time to help the patient withdraw gradually from addiction and achieve abstinence. In maintenance pharmacotherapy, the patient receives relatively stable doses of methadone on a sustained basis to maintain his or her normal physiological state, eliminating the uncontrolled craving for heroin and allowing a return to the normal activities of everyday life.

THE BALANCE BETWEEN TREATMENT AND PROHIBITION

The government's "war on drugs" has disproportionately emphasized the need to limit the availability of addictive substances, while restricting medical efforts to reduce demand. The Institute of Medicine suggests that a reallocation of priorities within the US Public Health Service could assign responsibility for oversight of methadone to a division more sensitive than DEA [Drug Enforcement Administration] to the balance between treatment and prohibition. . . . A medically oriented oversight agency could improve treatment services by helping clinics find better locations and allowing more flexibility to individualize treatment. Public acceptance could be enhanced by reporting the achievements of methadone clinics: termination of heroin use, social rehabilitation, reduction in criminal activity, improvement in health, and reduced transmission of hepatitis and acquired immunodeficiency syndrome.

Vincent P. Dole, *JAMA*, October 25, 1995.

For greatest effectiveness, methadone treatment should be coupled with a comprehensive package of health services and behavioral and social counseling, since addicts typically display a wide range of serious medical, psychological, economic, and legal problems in addition to their opiate dependence. It is also important to note that some—perhaps many—methadone-maintained patients will relapse into heroin use and will require readmission to treatment. But research has shown that, for many of these patients, the possibility of success increases with each additional period in treatment.

THE BENEFITS OF METHADONE

Once established in treatment, methadone-maintained patients show improvement in several outcomes. First, consumption of all illicit drugs declines. Numerous studies have found reductions in the frequency of heroin use to less than 40 percent on average of pre-treatment levels during the first year of treatment, and after two or more years heroin use declines to only 15 percent of pre-treatment levels. Second, there is a substantial drop in criminal behavior motivated by the addict's need to support his or her drug purchases. In a survey of 12 maintenance programs in three northeastern cities, for example, the crime rate dropped from a pre-treatment level of 237 "crime days" per year per 100 patients to 69 crime days—a reduction of more than 70 percent. Third, there is an improvement in public health, including the health of those who do not abuse drugs, especially with regard to reducing the transmission of the HIV virus and other infectious diseases, such as hepatitis and tuberculosis. In one study of AIDS rates, only 5 percent of methadone-maintained patients became infected (and only those who dropped out of the program contracted the virus) while an additional 26 percent of untreated opiate addicts became infected. Although these data do not prove that methadone was the causal agent generating the differences in infection rates, they do suggest that participation in maintenance pharmacotherapy was at least one factor in the reduction of such AIDS risk-reduction behaviors as needle sharing and sex-for-drugs transactions.

INCORRECT BELIEFS

The current regulations are predicated on a belief that the societal risks of methadone outweigh the societal benefits to such an extent that extraordinary controls are necessary. But our committee concluded that this belief is not valid in today's environment.

For one thing, research has yielded a rich understanding of the physiological mechanisms of opiate addiction and treatment. For example, opiate addiction is now understood to result not from personal weakness but from an interplay of physiological, psychological, social, and other variables. When a person takes heroin repeatedly, many of the body's organ systems adapt, or develop tolerance, to the opiate, which means that greater and greater doses are required to achieve the same effect. Once addicted, the person actually requires the drug to maintain physiological and psychological well-being.

Heroin and other addictive substances also seem to produce permanent changes in the physiology of biological systems, especially the brain, which may mediate the strong cravings for drugs that many addicted persons often experience even after years of abstinence. As Alan Leshner, director of the National Institute on Drug Abuse, often says, "Drug use is a choice, addiction is not." It is therefore appropriate to view addiction—including heroin, alcohol, and nicotine addiction—as a chronic relapsing medical condition that requires a variety of treatment strategies and management techniques, based on individual patient characteristics, in order to eliminate undesirable and dangerous social behavior.

In addition, we have learned more about the potential threat that methadone will be diverted from treatment programs to illicit street use. Although data from DEA and other agencies indicate that methadone has some potential for diversion and abuse, our committee concluded that experience has demonstrated that the actual diversion is quite small. Methadone has rarely been the preferred drug of abuse by users of illegal drugs—its action is too slow and the level of comfort it provides (particularly when taken orally, as it is used in treatment programs) is too mild. (As an indirect measure of methadone's lack of appeal on the street, there is no evidence that it has ever been the object of organized crime drug trafficking.) Most of the methadone diverted from licensed treatment programs appears to go to addicts who are trying to self-medicate, to patients who are getting inadequate doses of methadone in treatment, or to people seeking relief for a friend or family member in withdrawal. Our committee does, however, recommend careful monitoring of future diversion so that quick action can be taken to reinstate regulatory restrictions if a major health problem arises.

We have also learned more about the risks to society of heroin addiction—lessons that have come at great cost. While the risks associated with heroin addiction once seemed largely confined to the addicts themselves, it's now clear that this scourge is closely linked with increases in violent crime and the spread of deadly infectious diseases. Thus, methadone is no longer seen as a treatment designed to alleviate only the addict's problems, but also as a partial solution to a complex set of public health and safety issues.

"Plenty of things ... do appear to work [in fighting chemical dependency]—some simple, some complicated, and some novel."

A VARIETY OF APPROACHES CAN BE USED TO TREAT CHEMICAL DEPENDENCY

Joann Ellison Rodgers

Joann Ellison Rodgers is deputy director of public affairs and director of media relations for the Johns Hopkins Medical Institutions. She is also president of the Council for the Advancement of Science Writing, a lecturer in the Department of Epidemiology at the Johns Hopkins School of Hygiene and Public Health, and the author of numerous books and articles on medical issues. In the following viewpoint, Rodgers discusses several treatments that she says have proven to be effective for chemical dependency, including brief intervention, pharmacological treatment, and aversion therapy.

As you read, consider the following questions:
1. What is "warm turkey," and how can it help people fight chemical dependency, according to the author?
2. What are Ibogaine and Fen-Phen, and how do they work, according to Rodgers?
3. What is aversion therapy, as described by the author?

Addiction has no solitary cause. [Therefore], the new view toward it demands that single-minded approaches to drug treatment be abandoned. At least four studies, according to William Miller, Ph.D., a professor of psychology and psychiatry and director of the Center on Alcoholism, Substance Abuse, and Addictions at the University of New Mexico, have found no differences between groups of alcoholics assigned to Alcoholics Anonymous and to no treatment at all. AA simply doesn't work for a lot of people. Consistently negative findings have also come from controlled studies of insight-oriented psychotherapies, antipsychotic drugs, confrontational counseling, most forms of aversion therapy, educational lectures, group therapy, psychedelics, and hospitalization.

"A rather remarkable amount of research has been conducted on the effectiveness of several dozen approaches to the treatment of substance abuse," says Miller. But sadly, he says, the drug treatment community has been curiously resistant to using what works. His colleague, Reed Hester, after a review of treatment outcomes from 1980 to 1990, concluded that "despite much more knowledge of what works, treatment for substance abuse hasn't changed much in 40 years."

WHAT WORKS

Plenty of things, however, do appear to work—some simple, some complicated, and some novel. Some samples:

Brief intervention. According to Miller, studies show conclusively that very brief treatment, if designed properly, is highly successful against even moderately severe addictions.

"We found this out the hard way," he recalls. In 1976, in one of his studies of controlled drinking, Miller separated his subjects into two groups. The treatment group got a variety of treatments, including counseling and disulfiram (Antabuse). The control group was given only a brief self-help manual and told to go home, read it, and do their best.

"To our amazement, people in the control group did just as well as the treatment group. We thought we had really messed up the study so we repeated it twice again and got the same results.

"Then we went looking for what was really happening. We gave one group the manual and another group no manual. The manual turned out to be the variable that was the potent treatment. But why? We knew it wasn't the effect of our initial interview with the subjects, or some difference in the patient groups.

"The key was that we had inadvertently motivated the control group and in spite of our expectations, the addicts changed and moderated their drinking. Simply giving them the manual, saying to them that we believed they could help themselves, could handle it, you can do this, was enough."

Since then, Miller and other therapists have refined and modified "motivational interviewing" and brief-intervention therapy. More than 30 studies in 14 countries have affirmed the value of its key components, dubbed FRAMES: Feedback—specific and tailored to the individual, not general; Responsibility—it's up to you, your choice, you are not a helpless victim of a disease; Advice—firm and clear recommendations; Menu—there are different ways to work this out; Empathy—the best therapists have this and are neither pushy nor confrontational, but supportive and warm; and Self-efficacy—you can do it; empowerment.

"Warm turkey." Tapering down and "sobriety sampling" that give addicts a chance to kick their habits and help them not give up if they fail.

In the hands of trained therapists, this and other forms of "relapse prevention" teaches addicts skills for coping with mistakes and setbacks. These methods also allow for moderate continuation of some addictions for some people, rather than insisting on total abstinence.

DESIGNER DRUGS

Pharmacologic treatment. Drug treatments for addictions have historically been the least successful and the least available. Except for methadone (which many experts feel largely failed because accompanying social services and counseling were not given to addicts) and Antabuse for alcoholics, there has not been much to offer.

However, several groups of scientists are conducting studies looking for a methadone-style treatment for cocaine addiction. Now that neurobiologists and neurochemists have pinpointed those parts of the brain and the neurotransmitter system where cocaine exerts its effect, they plan to develop drugs that block it.

As Steven Childers, Ph.D., a physiologist and pharmacologist at Bowman Gray School of Medicine in North Carolina, explains: "Cocaine activates dopamine by inhibiting a mechanism that pushes dopamine back into nerve endings that release it. This pump, known as a dopamine transporter protein, is so inhibited by cocaine that dopamine is released in relatively huge amounts."

George Uhl, M.D., Ph.D., of the NIDA [National Institute on Drug Abuse] Addiction Research Center, and other scientists, using the gene cloned for the dopamine transporter protein, located specific areas where dopamine and cocaine both act in the brain.

Childers says the goal is to develop "designer drugs," man-made molecules that can block cocaine receptors without shutting down the dopamine transport system. (These are known as "antagonists" because they block the receptors.) Another strategy is to develop drugs that bind lightly to cocaine receptors, producing a very mild form of cocaine "rush" but also blocking cocaine itself. These drugs are known as mixed agonist/antagonists, or long-acting agonists.

TREATMENTS VARY

Substance abuse treatment programs differ in philosophy, setting, duration, and approach. Most involve some combination of detoxification, rehabilitation, continuing care (often called "aftercare") and relapse prevention. . . . As in other areas of medical treatment, there are several different "levels of care" which allow individuals to be treated at the most appropriate level of intensity.

U.S. Department of Health and Human Services, 1995.

Theoretically, says Childers, such drugs would break the behavioral-chemical links, the cycle that keeps cocaine addicts craving the drug. "We so far have only a long-acting agonist. That would still help clinically, the way methadone does, and those addicted to cocaine binges or overdoses would be helped. It might give a hard-core crack addict a way to come off his high slowly and perhaps not have the terrible withdrawal and craving."

IBOGAINE AND FEN-PHEN

Another pharmacologic approach that is drawing interest and controversy is the African hallucinogen ibogaine, made from the shrub *Tabernanthe iboga*, which grows in Gabon. Anecdotal evidence and a few animal studies suggest that ibogaine can cure opiate addictions. It's banned in the U.S., but a white powder made from it is available in Holland and many American junkies have gone abroad to get it.

Some patients claim it not only stops cravings for long periods without withdrawal, but also suppresses all desire for any drugs and generates an emotional confrontation with their own thoughts and feelings, during which they are inspired to reorganize their lives.

Scientists at NIDA say there is no evidence that it works, even over the long haul. Studies at Johns Hopkins have shown that ibogaine interrupts dopamine release and stimulates other neurotransmitters.

Still, most experts say the long-term effects reported by some users probably have more to do with the desire addicts have to kick their habits and to their expectation that it will work. At Johns Hopkins, Mark Molliver, M.D., and his team have also found ibogaine kills brain cells in a part of the brain—the orbital frontal cortex—linked to obsessive behavior. At present, neuroscientists at the University of Miami have the go-ahead to test ibogaine at low doses for safety, but not yet on addicts.

Then there's Fen-Phen, a pill containing an amphetamine cocktail made of fenfluramine and phentermine and widely used in recent years as a diet pill. A Maryland physician in private practice, Pietr Hitzig, M.D., claims the drug can stop alcoholism, cocaine addiction, sexual perversions, nail-biting, and a variety of other addictive behaviors, including compulsive eating. A four-year study conducted by Michael Weinraub, M.D., at the University of Rochester, has concluded that these drugs can help obese individuals lose and keep off weight.

In studies on monkeys, of one of Fen-Phen's components, however, dexfenfluramine, may produce lasting changes or damage in parts of the brain regulating appetite and mood.

SUDDEN CHANGES

Transformational psychology. The new view of addiction and some new ideas about treatment have been fed from such unusual sources as religion, philosophy, and literature. Recent research conducted on abrupt personality change is a case in point. The investigators, William Miller and Catherine Baca, M.D., of the University of New Mexico's Center on Alcoholism, Substance Abuse and Addictions, credit their study of Joan of Arc, Malcolm X, Alcoholics Anonymous cofounder Bill Wilson, Saint Paul, Buddha, Kierkegaard, and Dickens's *A Christmas Carol* for suggesting means by which some addicts might kick their habits overnight—much the way Ebenezer Scrooge went from wretched skinflint to kindly benefactor after a bad dream.

Whether or not their "transformational psychology" research translates into a practical treatment for addictive behavior, its publication by the American Psychological Association and presentation at international drug and alcohol research conferences reflect a shift in thinking about how people become addicted and how they might get free. Until now, says Miller, behavioral scientists have stuck to the conviction that real change, if it happens at all, is gradual and painstaking. Now, says Miller, we know that "relatively sudden and profound changes can and do occur, at least occasionally." If that capability could be harnessed, the impact on addiction could be profound.

Aversion therapy. Toni Farrenkopf uses aversion conditioning to treat addictions, particularly those involving gambling and sexual behavior. He's worked with patients for whom a single incident of voyeurism, or indecent exposure, sometimes at a very early age, was so arousing that the addiction held for decades.

"What we've learned is that people who are voyeurs and exposers are addicted to the rush they get from contemplating, planning, and doing the behavior, not necessarily from sexual release itself. With pedophiles, other factors drive the addiction. But in all cases, you want to try and countercondition the behavior."

TYING THE CONSEQUENCES TO THE BEHAVIOR

Aversive therapy works by introducing negative consequences immediately after the pleasurable experience occurs. One reason that many people don't become addicted is that they rarely experience the worst consequences of their behavior soon enough to override the pleasure.

Farrenkopf uses covert sensitization with imagery. He'll show a sexual addict arrest scenarios—being handcuffed, jailed, searched—10 seconds after an erotic exposure and do this repeatedly. Or he'll expose them to a noxious odor or painfully snap a rubber band on a wrist. "I help the patients experience all of the painful things that happen when they are caught, or have to confront their families after getting caught," he says. "It works for many."

In a related therapy for gamblers and others "addicted to thrills," Farrenkopf makes them do an inventory of how people are hurt by their behavior, and visualize how their family would feel if they were killed or maimed, how humiliating it would be for a professional to be arrested for drunk driving.

Behavioral shaping. A study by NIDA researcher Kenzie Preston, Ph.D., uses this method to ease inner-city cocaine addicts off the drug; they get increasing rewards in the form of redeemable vouchers to encourage abstinence. At the end of his first 12-week trial, nearly half the subjects had stayed free of coke for at least seven weeks. Among the rewards purchased with the vouchers: tennis shoes, tires, clothing, and a lawyer's fee.

| *"Anyone who recognizes [alcoholism] should be the one to confront it."*

INTERVENTIONS CAN HELP ALCOHOLICS

Jane E. Brody

Counselors frequently rely on interventions as a means of encouraging addicts to seek help. In an intervention, family members and friends confront the addict, explain how the addict's behavior has affected them, and strongly encourage the addict to accept help. In the following viewpoint, Jane E. Brody describes this process in detail and argues that interventions can be an effective way of forcing alcoholics to face and address their problem. Brody is a personal health columnist for the *New York Times*.

As you read, consider the following questions:
1. How did the intervention described in the viewpoint affect Stewart O., according to Brody?
2. What are some of the signs that someone is a problem drinker, according to the author?
3. According to Brody, how are the signs of alcoholism different for older adults?

S tewart O. did not seem like an alcoholic, at least not to those who worked with him. He was reliable and caring as a special education teacher during the school year and as a camp counselor every summer. But his friends and family saw another side of Stewart, an ugly, argumentative side that emerged when he had too much to drink, which seemed to be happening more and more often.

So they hatched a plan they hoped would save him. Everyone who meant anything to Stewart, including his 10- and 13-year-old children, joined him at a friend's house one morning on a ruse that they would be helping the friend move. Before Stewart knew what was happening, he found himself surrounded by a circle of caring friends and relatives who told him one by one that they loved him but could not continue to live with him or be his friend the way he was.

TOUGH LOVE

As one of his closest friends recalled, it was a show of tough love. He said he told Stewart: "I love you like a brother, but I need you to be different. I can't stand you when you're drunk. You get nasty, belligerent, hard to talk to. You put yourself and others in danger by driving drunk. You had an accident last month in which you could have been killed. I don't want to lose you. I want you to get help, and I want you to get it now. I have the names of people you can call who can help you."

Stewart was stunned, and so overwhelmed by this show of deep caring and concern that he wept. He also stopped drinking that very day. That was 13 years ago, and Stewart O., who asked that he not be further identified, has been dry ever since. He gives thanks daily for those who cared enough to save him from himself and give him back his life.

A HUGE HIDDEN PROBLEM

There are 18 million alcoholics in this country—men, women, teenagers, college students, the elderly—many of whom drink excessively in secret. At least they think it is in secret. Among them are people who are your neighbors, co-workers, friends or relatives. Chances are you know who at least some of them are, and chances are you are reluctant to interfere. You are afraid to embarrass the person or yourself, perhaps, or you are not sure what to say or do, or you think that surely someone closer to the person should be the one to intervene.

But experts who treat alcoholism say otherwise. Those closest are often the last to acknowledge the existence of alcoholism, perhaps because it happened gradually, perhaps because they are in perpetual denial. Rather, the experts insist, anyone who recognizes the problem should be the one to confront it, to call the person's attention to the fact that someone knows his or her "secret" and to let the person know that help and a listening ear are available whenever he or she is ready for them.

HOW TO INTERVENE

Recovery often begins when people stop rescuing the alcoholic. For example, don't provide the alcoholic with money to support the addiction or to help solve a related crisis. Don't call the alcoholic's employer to offer excuses for absences. . . .

To prepare for an intervention, gather those people who most affect the alcoholic's self-image—immediate family, close friends, an employer and/or a clergy person. Meet to write down and rehearse personal accounts of how the alcoholic has hurt them. It is very helpful to have an addictions counselor present. Follow these three guidelines for an intervention:

• Choose a place and time when the alcoholic is sober enough to comprehend what is being said.

• Provide some facts that link the drinker to an unpleasant situation or a crisis. For example, you can say: "Your employer called again today and wanted to know why you are sick so often."

• Be nonjudgmental. Convey love, concern and hope for the alcoholic. . . .

During the intervention, the alcoholic may become angry or remorseful. Several members of the group should be prepared to drive the alcoholic directly to a chemical dependency treatment center. (Be sure that you've called ahead to confirm there is space for your loved one.) If this attempt fails, never give up hope, addictions counselor Carol O'Reilly says. "Tell yourself, 'OK, it didn't work this time. But we're going to try it again.'" Then follow through with any ultimatums that you established during the intervention.

Brenda Shoss, *Safety & Health*, April 1996.

As Renee Zito, executive director of the Hazelden Fellowship Club, a chemical dependency treatment center in New York City, put it: "Say something, anything, to them. Let them know you're aware they have a problem. Sit them down and tell them: 'I love you too much to watch you die. I know there's help available and I want you to do something.' They may get furious with you and fly into a rage. But they will remember what you said at some level. Their denial will be pierced. They may not act on it right away, but if and when they do get help, they'll be grateful to you. They will recognize it as evidence that you care."

It does not matter if you say things imperfectly as long as you say something that expresses your concern with love, gentleness, and respect. Ms. Zito suggests using "I" phrases like "I noticed" or "I'm worried" since the person cannot argue with your feelings. She also suggests focusing on the effects alcohol abuse are having on whomever or whatever the person cares most about, whether it is a job, family, friends or physical or mental abilities.

RECOGNIZING THE SIGNS

How often a person drinks or how much that person consumes is not a reliable guide to the presence of an alcohol addiction problem. Nor can one rely on conventional stereotypes associated with late-stage alcoholism, like unreliability at work or as a spouse or parent, slovenliness, depleted finances or the presence of an alcohol-induced illness. The time to confront the problem is before it has had a devastating effect on a person's relationships, job and health.

The Hazelden Foundation, based in Center City, Minnesota, has published two brochures to help people detect alcohol or drug dependency in people they know and guide them through the intervention process. Among signs of alcohol abuse are these behaviors:

- Drinking more than usual, even if the increase occurred gradually.
- Periodically going on the wagon or switching from hard liquor to beer.
- Only going to parties or places where alcohol is available.
- Having a personality change when drinking.
- Driving after drinking or getting angry when you ask for the keys.
- Making calls late at night without remembering the conversation the next day.
- Bragging about drinking exploits or, if you do not approve, being secretive and withdrawn.
- Having a couple of drinks before you even get together.
- Complaining about other people or stopping seeing certain friends.
- Having problems on the job, at home, with money or with the law.

OLDER ADULTS

In older adults, the Hazelden experts say, the signs of alcoholism tend to be different. About two-thirds of older alcoholics have been drinking excessively for much of their adult lives, while the remaining third began abusing alcohol later in life, perhaps after retiring or losing a spouse.

Some of the signs of alcoholism in older people, like problems with memory, balance or sleep, are often incorrectly assumed to be a natural consequence of aging or the effects of chronic illness. Among other signs of alcohol abuse are these behaviors:

- Trying to dispose of large numbers of empty alcohol bottles secretly.
- Often seeming slightly tipsy or sometimes having slurred speech.
- Having unexplained burns or bruises and trying to hide them.
- Seeming more depressed or hostile than usual.
- Neglecting personal appearance or gaining or losing weight.
- Losing interest in activities or hobbies that he or she once enjoyed.
- Having trouble handling routine chores or paperwork.
- Having irrational fears or delusions or is unduly stressed.
- Often smelling of alcohol or the mouthwash used to disguise it.
- Complaining of sleeplessness, loss of appetite or other health problems that have no physical cause.
- Making a ritual of drinking before, with or after dinner and getting upset when this routine is disturbed.

| "For these troubled adolescents, . . .
AA seems to offer a haven of
empathy and acceptance."

ALCOHOLICS ANONYMOUS CAN HELP TEENAGE ALCOHOLICS

Beth Baker

Alcoholics Anonymous (AA), an international fellowship of recovering alcoholics, is probably the most well known alcoholic
treatment organization. In the following viewpoint, writer Beth
Baker explains how AA can help teenagers with alcohol problems. Baker explains that in the past teenagers have not commonly attended AA, but increasing numbers of them are now
using the organization to successfully address their problems
with alcohol.

As you read, consider the following questions:

1. What problems do some adults in AA have with teenagers
   who attend meetings, according to Baker?
2. Why do some people oppose court-ordered attendance at AA
   meetings, according to the author?
3. Why are many young people unwilling to attend AA, in
   Baker's opinion?

Beth Baker, "Stepping into Adulthood, " *Common Boundary*, September/October 1996.
Reprinted by permission of the author.

"**H**i. My name is Andrea, and I'm an alcoholic," says the young blond woman.

"Hi, Andrea," responds a motley chorus of teenagers slouched in metal chairs at a church in Bethesda, Maryland.

In her black baseball cap emblazoned with a skull, tight black jeans, and bright red lipstick, Andrea presents an incongruous image as she grapples aloud with whether or not she has reached Step 3 of the Alcoholics Anonymous (AA) Twelve Step program—turning her will and her life over to God. Andrea thought she had, but her AA sponsor told her otherwise. "How do we know if we've turned our lives over to a Higher Power?" Andrea wonders.

As at other Twelve Step meetings, participants at this young people's AA meeting offer their individual stories with little feedback or spiritual guidance from the group. Yet for these troubled adolescents, who testify to dysfunctional families, destructive relationships, unwanted pregnancies, and heavy substance abuse, AA seems to offer a haven of empathy and acceptance. "I barely know most of you, but you really help me make the right decisions, compared to the guys who've known me since I was in the crib," says one young man.

YOUNGER THAN EVER

AA describes itself as a fellowship of men and women who seek to recover from alcoholism by sharing their common experiences and problems. As part of the recovery process, members pursue a 12-step program based on spiritual growth, forgiveness, and prayer. As the organization celebrated its 60th anniversary in 1995, its membership had a younger face than ever before. In 1974, 8 percent of AA members were 30 years old or younger, and its membership survey did not reflect teens as a separate category. In the 1992 survey, 19 percent were 30 or younger, including 2 percent under 21.

"There are so many more young people in AA, compared to when I first started coming in 1977," says Cathy, who lives in the Atlanta suburbs. (AA members have a policy of using only their first names when interviewed and stress that their opinions are their own and do not represent those of the organization.) In many cities, AA now holds meetings primarily for young people. AA's General Service Office in New York City, which acts as a loose-knit national headquarters, distributes a video for teens as well as a number of brochures including "Young People and AA," "Too Young?", and "A Message for Teenagers . . . How to Tell When Drinking Is Becoming a Problem."

"It used to be that people in AA were more grown-up than teenagers, and its atmosphere reflected some intolerance," says George Vaillant, a professor of psychiatry at Harvard Medical School. "For AA to be meaningful, you need to be able to identify with other people in the group. To include young people is part of the natural expansion of AA, just as there are meetings for gay people, for airline pilots, or for African Americans."

DIFFICULTY IN RELATING

While some meetings have been established for young people, other general meetings have ended up attracting a large number of teens. At times, this situation poses a problem for adults who find it difficult to relate to younger people who abuse not only alcohol but also a virtual pharmacopeia of drugs. Frank talk about promiscuous behavior and frequent use of profanity can also be unsettling. According to Lee, office manager of the AA office in Washington, D.C., some older people have dropped out of meetings that became dominated by youths and have found other meetings where they felt more at home.

Ironically, young people are coming to AA in increasing numbers at a time when youthful imbibing may be on the decline. While data on teen alcoholism per se is scarce, the University of Michigan's annual Monitoring the Future Study found that 5.7 percent of high-school seniors drank daily in 1975, compared with 2.5 percent in 1993; 36.8 percent were "binge drinkers" in 1973, indulging in five or more drinks at a time, compared with 28.2 percent in 1994. Other studies that include younger teens, however, present a possible challenge to this finding. Geary Alford, a clinical psychologist and a professor at the University of Mississippi Medical Center, notes a lack of hard data, but on the basis of his experience counseling and conducting research in the field, he believes that teens are abusing substances at a younger and younger age.

REASONS FOR THE UPSURGE

While the data on teen alcoholism may be unclear, the upsurge in youthful AA membership is not. "I assume it's an indication that society is more open to the idea that alcoholism is a disease and not a moral weakness," says AA member Cathy.

Vaillant believes that many young people have a growing dependence on alcohol, one that is different from heavy social drinking. "It's got to do with feelings of despair and powerlessness," says Vaillant. "If you only get drunk when you want to, you're not likely to go to AA."

Young people with drinking problems are also more apt to be referred—in some cases, ordered—to AA meetings than they were in the past. According to the 1992 AA survey, 29 percent of all members were self-motivated to join AA. Young people are perhaps more likely to be represented in the other categories: the 27 percent who came from treatment facilities, the 21 percent who were pressured by families to come, or the 8 percent who were ordered by the courts to attend AA.

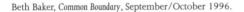

PERCENTAGE OF AA MEMBERS 30 YEARS OLD OR YOUNGER

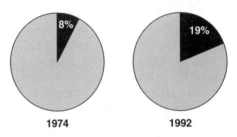

1974   1992

Beth Baker, *Common Boundary*, September/October 1996.

Some question the wisdom of courts ordering young people to attend AA, a supposedly voluntary self-help group, as if it were a form of punishment. One mother of a teenager in Bethesda, Maryland, reports that her son, who is not an alcoholic, was ordered by a judge to attend 60 AA meetings in a 90-day period. The 17-year-old boy (who declined to be interviewed) had been caught four times with beer, although he insisted he was actually drinking on only one of those occasions.

"He felt it did him no good to be in the [AA] program. Everyone assumed he was an alcoholic without really checking into his life," says his mother, who would have preferred that he be required to perform community service. Her son felt resentment from others at the meeting, who knew, because of a form he had to have signed, that he was there under compulsion.

NO COMPLAINTS

Judge Douglas Moore, who is in charge of the Juvenile Division of Maryland District Court in Montgomery County, says he often compels teenagers to go to AA or other substance-abuse programs. Typical cases involve teens who have committed an alcohol-related offense, such as driving while intoxicated, or who have been caught with possession of alcohol. "Even if they're not alcoholics, they can get something out of the program," says Moore. "They need some type of education to convince them they cannot drink legally and that there are hazards to drinking." He adds that he has never received complaints from AA about court-ordered attendance.

Monica Baker, a staff member at Good Shepherd, a residential treatment facility for adolescent girls in Baltimore, says that AA attendance, while helpful for some of her young charges, was also more of a lark for others, who saw it as a way to escape from the center for a couple of hours. "They were going to AA to socialize and talk about when they got drunk—but not in a therapeutic manner," says Baker. "They were there to play."

Older AA members, she adds, began to complain about the disruption. Some of the girls were asked to leave because of their behavior, despite AA's policy of keeping meetings open to all. As a result, girls at Good Shepherd must now show more evidence of alcoholism before attending AA.

While some young people may inappropriately wind up at AA, those teen alcoholics who have the most to gain are often unwilling to attend meetings. Alford finds that rebellious adolescents are a tough sell. "There's a goody-goody quality to AA," says Alford. "I'm saying that in a positive way. It stresses honesty, reconciliation, spirituality, a lifestyle of honor and truth. Some young adults see that as kind of wimpish and straight-laced, and it's a turn-off."

Young alcoholics who haven't hit bottom may not feel the urgency to turn their lives around. They haven't, for example, lost jobs or destroyed marriages. "If you're still thinking you're having fun drinking, you're probably not going to take AA seriously," says Lee. "Until a person believes that their problem is life-and-death, they're not going to stay sober."

A Success Story

One AA success story is Jeremy, a 22-year-old in Atlanta. He began drinking at age 12, became heavily involved in drugs, and grew suicidal. "I can't say that I felt invincible," Jeremy recalls. "I used to say I was too scared to kill myself. I couldn't imagine living, doing what I was doing, but I couldn't imagine living not doing what I was doing."

When Jeremy was 17, his father took him to a treatment center as a way to hide him from a vengeful drug dealer Jeremy had robbed. By the time he left the center, he had made up his mind to try AA. Five years later, he remains sober. By contrast, says Jeremy, the other teens with him in the treatment program did not join AA, and they continued drinking. Jeremy says that, in general, teens he knew were not serious about abstaining. He preferred attending AA meetings with older people, who could offer more in the way of advice and experience.

MATURITY AND INSIGHT

Alford, who conducted one of the few studies on the effectiveness of AA for adolescents, believes that the organization's approach holds promise for young people. He and his colleagues followed 157 teenagers who had been in an inpatient treatment program based on the AA model. Six months after their release, about three-quarters of the youths were "abstinent or essentially abstinent." After a two-year follow-up, the number of abstainers had dropped to 40 percent. Of the group who continued to attend AA each week, however, 84 percent were abstinent.

Many of the youth who attend the young people's AA meeting in Bethesda, Maryland, clearly are benefiting from the support they find there. While much of their testimony is scattered, hostile, and confused, many of the participants show maturity and insight. "No matter how much other people have hurt me, it's nothing compared to how I hurt myself," says one young woman, to many nodding heads.

Another, Sara, describes an adolescence filled with drugs, booze, and domineering men. She ran away from home and worked in a strip joint in Texas. Her father, himself an alcoholic, finally sat her down and told her, "You're an alcoholic. It's not your fault, but it's your responsibility." For Sara, the words struck a strong chord. While she doesn't claim the road was easy, she seems well on her way to recovery.

Once a young person such as Sara acknowledges that he or she is an alcoholic, AA can be a powerful motivator to remain sober in the face of tremendous social pressure to drink. Says Jeremy: "I heard from older guys that I was too young to be an alcoholic, but they didn't know me or know what's inside my head."

Jeremy is now an AA sponsor not only for younger people but also for those much older. He takes AA to the county jail and holds meetings with inmates. "Most of the people my age aren't into what I'm into," he says. "I'm into living and God." He adds with a laugh, "You know—doing things that aren't too cool."

> "Moderation Management . . . provide[s] a supportive environment in which people who have made the healthy decision to reduce their drinking can come together to help each other change."

THE PRINCIPLES OF MODERATE DRINKING CAN HELP PROBLEM DRINKERS

Audrey Kishline

Audrey Kishline is the founder and president of Moderation Management, a network of self-help groups for problem drinkers who want to moderate their drinking rather than abstain from alcohol. In the following viewpoint, Kishline contends that the standard treatment given to alcoholics—being labeled an alcoholic and required to give up alcohol—is ineffective for some problem drinkers. Kishline believes that such drinkers can learn to moderate their drinking and gain control of the problems excessive drinking can cause.

As you read, consider the following questions:

1. What are the author's credentials for writing about alcohol problems?
2. How does Moderation Management work, according to Kishline?
3. What four reasons does Kishline give to explain the need for Moderation Management?

One afternoon, as I was driving home on the freeway, a question crossed my mind. It went something like this:

There are thousands of support groups available in our country for chronic drinkers who have made the decision to abstain from alcohol. Why aren't there any support groups available for problem drinkers who have made the decision to reduce their drinking? . . . Chronic drinkers are people who are severely dependent on alcohol and, due to a high tolerance, usually experience withdrawal symptoms if they stop drinking. Their histories of harmful drinking are frequently long, in the range of 10 years or more. They usually have had many alcohol-related crises in their lives, are in poor health, and have few personal, social, and economic resources left. Problem drinkers, on the other hand, do not experience significant withdrawal symptoms when they stop drinking. Their problem drinking histories are usually shorter, often five years or less. And, significantly, problem drinkers normally still have most of their life resources intact and possess the skills and tools necessary for self-change.

When I finally realized why there were no support groups available for problem drinkers, I became very upset. Then, after I calmed down, I . . . started a support group called Moderation Management (MM) for problem drinkers who want to moderate their drinking behavior. . . .

MODERATION MANAGEMENT CAN HELP

Now I have a few questions for you: Is drinking too much beginning to cause problems in your life? Do you really want to change this behavior and reduce the amount you drink? Do you accept full responsibility for your own actions? If so, then I believe that the program and support groups of Moderation Management can help you achieve your goals.

I firmly believe this for several reasons. The basic concepts of MM are derived from brief behavioral self-management approaches to alcohol abuse, which in turn are based on research—controlled studies and clinical trials with problem drinkers. These methods are currently being used successfully with problem drinkers in formal treatment and educational programs. The guidelines toward moderation and positive lifestyle changes . . . have been carefully reviewed by professionals in the field, including physicians, psychiatrists, psychologists, social workers, and substance abuse educators. But most importantly, the program of MM was born from the real-life experiences of former problem drinkers who have returned to moderate drinking, including myself.

I will now provide you with my "credentials" as a former problem drinker. Though this is something I would prefer not to do, it is necessary because there are those who believe that a return to moderate drinking is impossible for anyone who has ever had a drinking problem. They will say that I never was an "alcoholic." And they are correct, if by "alcoholic" they mean a chronic, severely dependent drinker. But if by "alcoholic" they mean a person with any type of drinking problem (including mild to moderate levels of alcohol-related problems), then saying I was never an "alcoholic" would imply that I never had a "real" drinking problem—in which case, they are wrong.

I started out like many other people. I first tried alcohol in my late teens at home, and began drinking socially in my early twenties with friends. From my early to late twenties, however, over a period of about six years, I gradually drank more, and more often. Drinking eventually became a central activity in my life: the people I associated with were mostly heavy drinkers, my evenings were planned around drinking, and having fun meant alcohol had to be involved.

Alcohol became a way to cope with life—the ups, the downs, and "in-betweens." I drank when I was happy, when I was sad, when I was bored, or when I didn't know how I was feeling. But mostly I drank because it became a habit. (And I have read that there are probably as many reasons why drinking becomes a habit in the first place as there are problem drinkers.) Naturally this way of acting, which I call a bad habit, and the psychologists prefer to describe as a "maladaptive behavior," began to cause problems in my life.

I did not feel well physically, did not eat right, and slept poorly. I drank daily, the amounts gradually increasing, hangovers becoming more frequent. I did not perform to the best of my abilities at work, and began to have difficulties keeping up with courses I was taking in night school. I started to postpone everything: studying, projects, hobbies, even getting together with people I knew did not drink as much as I did. I drank irresponsibly, risking other people's lives when I drove after I had too much. Finally, after a long-term relationship fell apart, I started to drink alone. I became depressed, scared, and lonely.

TRADITIONAL TREATMENT

I decided to seek help. For those who say I was never an "alcoholic," I want to stress that two treatment centers, an aftercare program, and conservatively 30 to 40 professionals—including physicians, psychiatrists, psychologists, social workers, and certified substance abuse counselors—had no problem saying that I was. Nor did they have any difficulty accepting payment for the "treatment" I received. . . .

So, with my new "alcoholic" label, I experienced traditional treatment firsthand. For my "medical disease" I received the following treatment for 28 days as a "patient" on the third floor of a hospital: group psychotherapy, confrontational counseling, life-skills training, therapeutic duties (e.g., making beds, cleaning bathrooms), and a daily vitamin pill. My "detoxification" consisted of sleeping in a room separate from the rest of the clients where a nurse could take my blood pressure and temperature regularly for 24 hours. It is important to note that I *did not experience any significant withdrawal symptoms when I quit drinking.* This indicated that my physical dependence on alcohol was not severe—a point either ignored or considered irrelevant by treatment personnel.

MODERATE DRINKING: AN APPROPRIATE GOAL

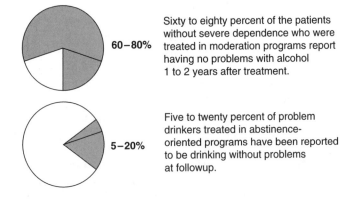

60–80% Sixty to eighty percent of the patients without severe dependence who were treated in moderation programs report having no problems with alcohol 1 to 2 years after treatment.

5–20% Five to twenty percent of problem drinkers treated in abstinence-oriented programs have been reported to be drinking without problems at followup.

Katharine A. Bradley, *Alcohol Health & Research World*, Spring 1994.

In addition, I was introduced to the institutionalized version of Alcoholics Anonymous (AA) and forced to attend meetings on a daily basis while still in the hospital. I use the term "forced" because I was informed that if I did not comply I would not "graduate" from their program, and my insurance would not cover my (expensive) treatment. . . .

CHOOSING TO DRINK

The result of all this "treatment"? At first, my drinking became far worse. Hospital staff members had told me that I had a physical disease that I had no control over, a condition that was inevitably progressive. Further, they had told me that I was an "alcoholic" for whom AA was the only cure; and in AA I learned that "alcoholics of their type" were powerless over alcohol. I kept hearing "one drink, one drunk," "once an alcoholic, always an alcoholic," and that "alcohol is cunning, baffling, and powerful." In possibly the most defenseless and dependent stage of my entire life, I began to fulfill some of these prophecies. I became a binge drinker, suddenly obsessed with either drinking too much or not at all. I felt disgraced and demoralized, forever branded with the "alcoholic" label that became my entire identity. I ended up accepting that I was indeed powerless over my "condition," and my old self-esteem and confidence gradually disappeared.

Then, as time passed, I began to do what a lot of other people do naturally, *with or without treatment*. I began to grow up. I matured, and took on life's responsibilities. I got married, had children, and became a full-time homemaker. I took courses in college again, developed a few new hobbies and other interests, and made new friends. Though initially *told* to stop drinking, I eventually *chose* to abstain from alcohol entirely for long periods of time after treatment. (Like many former problem drinkers, I believe that an initial abstinence period—step two of the MM program—is important in order to lower any increased physical tolerance to alcohol, reestablish priorities, and work on life skills that were not developed while drinking excessively.) It gradually dawned on me that the choice to abstain or the choice to drink, and how much to drink, had been mine to make all along. These choices were not predetermined by a disease at all, but were entirely a result of my own decisions, which I did have control over. So . . . I decided to shed my "disease." And I took back full responsibility for my own behavior.

Several years ago, after careful consideration, I made the choice to return to moderate drinking. By "moderate drinking" I do not mean white-knuckled, super-controlled, "I really want more" drinking, as is often described by those who don't believe this is possible. I mean that I am comfortable with the role that alcohol plays in my life now. When I choose to drink, I drink in moderation and responsibly. An occasional glass of wine is a small, though enjoyable, part of my life—not the center of my life. And alcohol no longer stops me from doing more important things with my time, like living every day to its fullest. . . .

THE PURPOSE OF MM

The purpose of Moderation Management is to provide a supportive environment in which people who have made the healthy decision to reduce their drinking can come together to help each other change. That's it. It is very simple and straightforward, and I admit that MM stole it from the forerunner of the mutual help movement, AA. The idea of people getting together to help other people who have, or have had, similar problems is an old but good one. Problem drinkers who want to change, and former problem drinkers who want to maintain the positive changes that they've made, attend MM meetings to achieve a balanced way of life not only where alcohol is concerned, but in other areas as well.

How does MM accomplish its purpose? First of all, the meetings themselves are free; there are no dues or fees charged by MM support groups. So if you want help, it will be within your budget. But remember that the meetings are led by and made up of volunteers who are not alcohol abuse counselors and who do not give professional advice (which is one reason why the meetings are free). What members do offer, however, is very effective.

People who have had problems with alcohol have *been there*—they can empathize, sympathize, and offer suggestions. And they can *be there*—to motivate, to encourage, and to listen. One of the most important ways in which MM meetings help problem drinkers is through the power of example, the real-life example of former problem drinkers who have turned their lives around. People who are beginning the program also receive support from each other because they are working on the same type of problem at the same time. "Oldtimers" and "newcomers" alike are encouraged when they see other members develop self-confidence and gradually achieve self-defined goals. The members are the strength of the MM program.

NINE STEPS

MM also offers a set of professionally reviewed guidelines, the Nine Steps Toward Moderation and Positive Lifestyle Changes. They are at the center of the program, providing structure and a means for members to follow their progress. The steps include information about alcohol, empirically based moderate drinking limits, self-evaluation exercises, drink monitoring forms, self-management strategies, and goal-setting techniques. (Those who do not feel that they need the extra support of a group, or who are uncomfortable in group settings, can use [the MM guidebook] alone for information about moderate drinking guidelines.)

Step two of the program suggests that members abstain from alcohol for 30 days. This allows members to experience a substantial period of abstinence before going on to the moderation part of the program, and it helps them to make an informed choice between moderation and abstinence. Those who are able to moderate their drinking behavior find that the initial abstinence period strengthens their commitment to change. Those who find moderation more difficult to maintain than abstinence can choose to go on to an abstinence-based program rather than remain in MM, and the groups will provide such people with information on abstinence-oriented groups.

MM's steps are not set in concrete or divinely inspired, but they have many positive aspects: they make "common sense"; they are based on the experience of former problem drinkers; and they have been carefully reviewed by professionals in the addictions field. The purpose of the steps is to help you achieve moderation, but they might as well be written in Greek if you do not think that you have a problem with alcohol or are not motivated to change. . . .

You have to acknowledge that you have a problem with alcohol ("self-identify" as a problem drinker) and you have to decide whether you want to do something about it. Then MM can assist you by providing a suggested plan of action (the nine steps of the program), group support while you put the plan into action, and continued support when (or if) you need help to maintain the changes you've made.

WHY WE NEED MM

We need a support group network like Moderation Management for several reasons. First, problem drinkers are more likely to seek help from a support group that they believe fits their needs than from one that doesn't. Second, they will seek help *sooner* from a program that specifically addresses the concerns of problem drinkers rather than those of chronic drinkers. Third, there are far more problem drinkers than severely dependent drinkers in our country. And fourth, until now there have been no widely available support groups that offer the option of moderation. (At the time of this writing, MM is not yet widely available— but new MM groups are forming each month in cities across the country.) . . .

The majority of adults in our country drink, and for the most part they drink responsibly. There are also some perceived and actual advantages to drinking moderately. People choose to drink because it is relaxing, enhances socializing, and can add to a special occasion. Medical research has confirmed that the moderate consumption of alcohol can even be beneficial to one's health because it significantly lowers rates of heart disease.

Of course, it would be nice (in fairy tale land) if everyone could be "high on life" all of the time and never resort to using food (ice cream sundaes) or other mood-altering substances. But how many people do you know who drink coffee in the morning to help them get going? Why aren't they all out jogging to get their eyes opened? How many people do you know who occasionally have a glass of wine to relax after work? Why aren't they all doing a half-hour of yoga to wind down instead? And why can't I eat a tofu salad with as much gusto as I eat chocolate cake?

Most people have at least some bad habits. Not many of us are marathoning, herbal tea drinking, nonsmoking, non-drinking, reed-thin demigods. So what is the answer? In a nutshell, it is to take stock of wherever you are now, and to try to change for the better—maybe with the support of other people who have, or have had, problems similar to your own. The solution to doing too much of something is not always another extreme (quitting altogether). Many times the solution lies somewhere between the extremes, and it is called moderation.

PERIODICAL BIBLIOGRAPHY

The following articles have been selected to supplement the diverse views presented in this chapter. Addresses are provided for periodicals not indexed in the *Readers' Guide to Periodical Literature*, the *Alternative Press Index*, the *Social Sciences Index*, or the *Index to Legal Periodicals and Books*.

Addiction Letter	"Family Therapy Works for Drug Abuse," January 1996. Available from Mannisses Communication Group, Box 9758, Providence, RI 02940-9758.
William J. Bennett and John P. Walters	"Drugs: Face the Facts, Focus on Education," *Insight*, March 6, 1995. Available from 3600 New York Ave. NE, Washington, DC 20002.
Jerry E. Bishop	"Doctors Are High on Battling 'Crack,'" *Wall Street Journal*, March 17, 1995.
Lee Brown	"It Can Be Won—with the Right Treatment," *World & I*, June 1995. Available from 3600 New York Ave. NE, Washington, DC 20002.
Emily Carter	"I Fought the Hardest Battle of My Life—and Won," *Family Circle*, March 14, 1995.
Paul Cotton	"'Harm Reduction' Approach May Be Middle Ground," *JAMA*, June 1, 1994. Available from AMA, Library, 515 N. State St., Chicago, IL 60610.
James W. Langenbucher	"Socioeconomic Analysis of Addictions Treatment," *Public Health Reports*, March/April 1996.
A. Thomas McLellan, George E. Woody, and David Metzger	"Evaluating the Effectiveness of Addiction Treatments: Reasonable Expectations, Appropriate Comparisons," *Milbank Quarterly*, Spring 1996.
Jill Neimark, Claire Conway, and Peter Doskoch	"Back from the Drink," *Psychology Today*, September/October 1994.
Charles P. O'Brien and A. Thomas McLellan	"Myths About the Treatment of Addiction," *Lancet*, January 27, 1996. Available from 655 Avenue of the Americas, New York, NY 10010.
Linda Piwowarski	"Does Your Parish Have a Drinking Problem?" *U.S. Catholic*, June 1995.
Nicholas A. Seivewright and Judy Greenwood	"What Is Important in Drug Misuse Treatment?" *Lancet*, February 10, 1996.

CHAPTER 4

SHOULD DRUG LAWS
BE REFORMED?

CHAPTER PREFACE

The United States has thousands of laws that control, regulate, or prohibit the possession, use, and sale of drugs and alcohol. Federal spending on drug control programs alone was expected to amount to $15.1 billion in fiscal year 1997, up from $1.5 billion in 1981. These figures do not include the amount spent by state and local governments on drug control or the amount spent by all agencies on alcohol regulation.

Government efforts generally focus on reducing the supply of intoxicating substances or lowering the demand for such substances. Destroying marijuana crops and arresting cocaine smugglers are just two of the many ways of controlling the supply of drugs. Treating addicts and educating children on the hazards of substance abuse are two ways to reduce the demand.

Disagreement over government drug laws often focuses on the issues of supply and demand. Those who support reducing the supply of drugs often believe that drug treatment is ineffective and that the best way to stop drug abuse is to control people's access to drugs. "While drug treatment may help a small number of Americans to end their dependence on drugs, it cannot stop others from following them down the same path," argue Jeffrey A. Eisenach and Andrew J. Cowin. They conclude: "By contrast, a greater emphasis on law enforcement . . . would deter drug use before it started."

But opponents of this view argue that years of pouring money into supply-oriented measures such as law enforcement have been ineffective. Many commentators contend that rather than waging a "war on drugs," the government should provide treatment for drug abusers. "Drug rehabilitation . . . is the best government can do to reduce the public and social costs—that is, unless this nation is willing to build a prison in virtually every neighborhood," according to the *Los Angeles Times*.

In the following chapter, the authors debate whether drug laws are effective, fair, and helpful to addicted individuals and to society as a whole.

> "Because of the legal restrictions placed on the distribution and possession of certain drugs, infection, violence and criminal injustice leave death and destruction in their wake."

DRUGS SHOULD BE LEGALIZED

William London

Government efforts to curtail drug abuse through the arrest and imprisonment of drug users and dealers have resulted in disease, crime, and violence, William London writes in the following viewpoint. He argues that legalizing drugs would be a more effective means of addressing the drug problem. Legalization would enable the government to control the sale, distribution, and use of drugs, he contends, and would allow the nation to treat drug abuse as a public health issue instead of a criminal justice problem. London concludes that legalizing drugs would dramatically reduce the violence and other social ills that now result from the illegal drug trade. London is the director of public health for the American Council on Science and Health in New York City.

As you read, consider the following questions:

1. How does the author respond to the argument that drug use will increase if drugs are legalized?
2. How has the prohibition of drugs led to the spread of infectious diseases, according to London?
3. What does London mean when he says that drug dealers have the most to lose from legalization?

William London, "Will Legalizing Drugs Benefit Public Health?" *Priorities*, vol. 7, no. 2 (1995). Reprinted with permission from *Priorities*, a publication of the American Council on Science and Health, 1995 Broadway, 2nd Floor, New York, NY 10023-5860.

The "War on Drugs" has never been a carefully planned public health protection initiative. Government officials did not enact current drug prohibition laws and enforcement policies because of any dispassionate, comprehensive review of drug hazards. Rather, hysterical fear-mongering has always been the real basis for the "War on Drugs."

Wars require propaganda to maintain them, and the drug war is no exception. The names of propaganda groups such as Partnership for a Drug-Free America and the U.S. Department of Education (DOE)'s Drug-Free Schools and Communities Program imply that nothing short of a utopian outcome will suffice. Efforts to achieve a drug-free society through war have had less than utopian consequences, however; and those consequences are exemplified by the war's casualties—the victims of infection, violence and criminal injustice.

FAILED PROHIBITION EFFORTS

Federal drug prohibition began in the United States in 1914, when Congress passed a law to ensure the orderly marketing of narcotics: the Harrison Narcotic Act. The law responded to concerns about the cut-rate marketing of British opium in China and its effect on China's purchasing power for American products. The congressional debates on the act were concerned with international obligations, not with issues of public health.

To the surprise of many, law-enforcement officers and the courts interpreted the Harrison Act as highly restrictive. Physicians who prescribed opiates to addicts were arrested, convicted and imprisoned. Desperate for drugs, addicts found them available only through illegal channels. Thus, the association between drugs and crime was firmly established through acts of legislation and enforcement, not through the pharmacological actions of the drugs themselves.

The ratification of the 18th Amendment to the Constitution brought about the national prohibition of alcohol in 1920. Prohibition failed to live up to the widespread expectation of its producing an alcohol-free, slum-free, prison-emptied society. Instead, it encouraged the spread of organized crime and the corruption of public officials, overburdened the court and prison systems, made alcoholic beverages more dangerous to consume (black markets tend to lack appropriate manufacturing standards), removed a significant source of tax revenue and increased government spending.

The "noble experiment" of national alcohol prohibition ended with the ratification of the 21st Amendment in 1933.

However, a new experiment was initiated a scant four years later. Largely due to Harry Anslinger, Commissioner of the Bureau of Narcotics, who had shamelessly been promoting distorted horror stories of marijuana use, Congress passed the Marijuana Tax Act. The law banned the nonmedicinal, untaxed sale or possession of marijuana. At the congressional hearings on the act, there was no medical testimony favoring its passage; the only physician to testify opposed the bill.

Don Wright. Reprinted by permission: Tribune Media Services.

By 1988, in the spirit of "zero tolerance," federal law permitted, without even a semblance of due process, drug-enforcement agents to seize boats, cars and planes that contained even traces of marijuana.

PRINCIPLES OF SOUND PUBLIC HEALTH POLICY

Only rarely can we (or should we) try to *eliminate* health threats the way we have eliminated smallpox. The American Council on Science and Health has documented the folly of numerous public health laws, most notably the Delaney Clause of the Food, Drug, and Cosmetic Act, which tolerates zero risk from food additives regardless of their benefits. ACSH has appropriately promoted the reduction of harm from significant, high-priority, public health hazards, not the elimination of all purported hazards regardless of their public health significance.

Public health activists should guard against promoting "cures" whose consequences are worse than the "diseases" they address. In developing rational policies toward nonmedicinal use of drugs, Charles Murray's "Law of Net Harm" should be considered: "The less likely it is that the unwanted behavior will change voluntarily, the more likely it is that a program to induce change will cause net harm."

In the interest of promoting the greatest good for the greatest number of people, public health interventions may on some occasions limit personal autonomy. In these cases, however, there should always be compelling reasons for the intrusive interventions; and the degree of intrusion should be kept to a minimum.

Sometimes it may be prudent to have public policies that attempt to protect people from making the sort of unwise decisions that can cause harm to themselves. Seat-belt laws are possible examples. It is more important, however, to protect people from the dangerous behavior of others. The gunfire and societal mayhem resulting from drug prohibition endangers people who would never consider taking the prohibited drugs. . . .

DRUG HAZARDS IN PERSPECTIVE

Although legally sold to adults, one bundle of drugs, tobacco, kills more Americans (over 400,000 annually) than do alcohol and all other drugs combined. Excluding tobacco, alcohol kills more Americans (over 100,000 each year) than do these other drugs combined. American deaths from all other drugs are frequently estimated at about 10,000 per year, with over half of those deaths attributable to cocaine or heroin and none attributable to marijuana. . . .

Far more Americans die from the use of tobacco and the abuse of alcohol than die from abuse of other drugs—largely because far more Americans abuse tobacco and alcohol than abuse other drugs. About 25 percent of American adults, college students and high school students are current smokers. The *National Household Survey on Drug Abuse: Population Estimates 1992* showed, for the previous 30 days, 48 percent alcohol use, about four percent marijuana use and less than one percent use of cocaine, crack and heroin.

Defenders of drug prohibition may be tempted to argue that prohibition keeps the prevalence of drug use low and thereby limits drug-related morbidity and mortality. It is possible that the repeal of drug prohibition would lead to increased drug use, but I'm aware of no evidence that a large number of Americans are hoping that drugs will be legalized so that they can finally indulge in psychoactive recreations.

Prohibitionists' platitudes about "sending the wrong message" through legalization ignore, first, the dramatic decline in tobacco smoking since the 1960s—without our having instituted tobacco prohibition; second, the very small increase in the use of marijuana, a drug feared far less than cocaine and heroin, following decriminalization in Oregon in 1973; and, third, the expansion of cocaine use during the 1980s, even with no change in cocaine's legal status.

FACTORS THAT DETERMINE CONSEQUENCES

Increases (or decreases) in drug use do not in and of themselves have public health significance—because drug use in and of itself does not imply harmful consequences. The consequences of drug taking are determined by four factors: (1) the pharmacological actions at various doses, (2) the method of administration, (3) set and (4) setting.

(1) *Pharmacological actions.* "The dose makes the poison" may be the most important concept in pharmacology. Protecting people from small amounts of drugs can have no more than a small impact on public health. Most use of small amounts of drugs—with the notable exception of tobacco—does not lead to disease or addiction.

(2) *Method of administration.* Some methods of drug taking are more dangerous than others. Administration through injection, especially with shared needles, is potentially more dangerous than the drugs being injected.

(3) *Set* and (4) *Setting.* "Set" refers to the psychological and physical characteristics of the drug user. "Setting" refers to the social and physical environment in which drugs are used. The rarity of addiction to prescribed narcotics for postoperative pain illustrates the importance of both set and setting. Focusing on the drugs themselves to the exclusion of all else ignores potential opportunities for reducing harm by addressing these "host" and "environmental" factors.

Unlike readily available legal pharmaceuticals, the illegal drugs sold on the street are typically adulterated. By introducing standards of identity, purity, sterility and dosage, legalization can reduce the harmful potential of heroin and the other drugs currently sold on the black market.

If the prohibition of drugs is as necessary as its defenders claim to protect public health, why do so few people promote the prohibition of tobacco and alcohol, the major causes of behaviorally induced mortality in the United States? Perhaps the prohibitionists secretly recognize that expanding the "War on

Drugs" to include tobacco and alcohol would expand the number of war casualties.

CASUALTIES OF THE "DRUG WAR"

The number of casualties resulting from the "war" on drugs exceeds the number of casualties resulting from drug use. Because of the legal restrictions placed on the distribution and possession of certain drugs, infection, violence and criminal injustice leave death and destruction in their wake.

(1) *Infection.* Inflated drug prices resulting from the lack of a free market provide an incentive to buyers to use the efficient, yet dangerous, injection method to administer drugs. Through many years of syringe and needle prohibition, a culture of sharing the "works" has developed. But the sharing of needles and syringes speeds the spread of infectious diseases such as tetanus, hepatitis and AIDS. According to the Centers for Disease Control and Prevention (CDC), through December 1994 in the United States, there were 109,393 AIDS cases traceable to injecting drug use: 28,521 cases among men who have sex with men and inject drugs; 15,758 cases traceable to heterosexual contact with injecting drug users; and 3,376 pediatric AIDS cases for which the mother was at risk of infection through either injecting drug use or sex with an injecting drug user.

(2) *Violence.* Major drug dealers have more to lose than anyone from the legalization of drugs. Operating as they do outside free markets and without the burden of the taxes that legitimate businesspeople pay, black-market drug traffickers have opportunities for extraordinary profits.

A common business problem among dealers is the processing of enormous amounts of cash. As a consequence, dealers are usually well armed, both to protect themselves from those law-enforcement officers who are not on their payrolls and to blow away anyone else who crosses them. In countries such as Brazil, Peru, Mexico, Panama and Colombia, drug cartels, gangs and death-and-torture squads have murdered countless opponents of the illegal drug trade—including judges, journalists, political candidates and other citizens.

In any forceful response to drug terrorists, additional people—including innocent bystanders—inevitably die. For example, the American military's pursuit and capture of the former drug-trafficking tyrant of Panama, Manuel Noriega, killed over 200 civilians and over 300 soldiers. Hundreds of millions of U.S. dollars were spent on the invasion of Panama and Noriega's trial.

The ties between the drug trade and gangs are close ones. A

significant number of the 809 juveniles who were victims of gang slayings in the United States in 1992 were undoubtedly child casualties of the drug war. The U.S. Department of Justice conservatively estimated that 1,284 drug-related homicides occurred in the United States in 1992. Many of those victims were—and continue to be—people who never used drugs or associated with the drug trade but who happened to wind up in the line of fire, some of it from police.

In 1988, drug scams or disputes over drugs accounted for 18 percent of the defendants in murder cases in the nation's 75 most populous counties. It is unrealistic to expect armed drug dealers to handle their most difficult conflicts through legal channels.

(3) *Criminal Injustice.* Nevertheless, drug dealers and users of illegal drugs often do wind up in the criminal justice system. According to the U.S. Department of Justice, in 1992 there were about 980,700 adult arrests for drug offenses, up from 471,200 in 1980. That 1992 figure was larger than the same year's combined total of arrests for murder, rape, robbery, aggravated assault and burglary. In 1992 there were about 102,000 new court commitments for drug offenses, representing an estimated 30.5 percent of all new court commitments. That figure was up from 6.8 percent in 1980.

Clogged courts mean plea bargaining and reduced sentences for violent offenders—who are the real menaces to society. Overcrowded prisons expose nonviolent offenders convicted on drug charges to prison violence, epidemics of drug-resistant tuberculosis and other infectious diseases and the socialization influences of hardened criminals.

Prematurely releasing violent criminals to make room for nonviolent drug offenders sentenced to draconian mandatory minimum sentences is an outrageous assault on public health. Those who advocate imprisoning drug users (at a cost of about $20,000 per year per offender) are often strongly pro-family, but few events disrupt the functioning of a family—and thereby increase the risk for juvenile drug abuse—as much as a family member going to prison.

The term "War on Drugs" is a misnomer. It is not a war on inanimate objects, but a war on people. Its casualties of epidemic infection, corruption, torture, murder and incarceration far exceed the speculated casualties from drug abuse under any plausible, pessimistic, post-legalization scenario. The failure to heed the Hippocratic dictum "first, do no harm" in formulating drug policy has given us the longest, most destructive war in American history. It's time for peace.

"It is surprising that some people . . .
continue to bring up the issue of
legalizing marijuana and other illicit
drugs. That would be a huge mistake."

DRUGS SHOULD NOT BE LEGALIZED

Donna E. Shalala

Donna E. Shalala is the U.S. secretary of health and human services. In the following viewpoint, she argues that legalizing
drugs would send the message that drugs are not hazardous.
Consequently, she argues, more Americans would experiment
with and become addicted to drugs. Shalala suggests that a comprehensive antidrug strategy—including education, treatment,
and enforcement of drug laws—would be a more effective way
to fight drug abuse.

As you read, consider the following questions:
1. What are the dangers of marijuana use, according to Shalala?
2. What three reasons does Shalala give for her opposition to
   drug legalization?
3. Who can help the government combat drug abuse, in the
   author's opinion?

Donna E. Shalala, "Say 'No' to Legalization of Marijuana," *Wall Street Journal*, August 18,
1995. Reprinted with permission of the *Wall Street Journal*, ©1995 Dow Jones & Company,
Inc. All rights reserved.

In 1995, the Department of Health and Human Services held the first-ever national research conference on marijuana, at which scientists presented groundbreaking information about the danger of marijuana use. What was said has implications for every business, every citizen, and every parent, particularly as new calls are being heard to legalize marijuana.

Peter Fried, who is associated with Carleton University in Ottawa, discussed his preliminary findings that marijuana use during pregnancy has harmful effects on children's intellectual abilities a decade or more after they are born. Through the use of an animal model of addiction, Billy Martin of Virginia Commonwealth University showed that compulsive marijuana use may lead to an addiction similar to those produced by other illicit drugs.

These findings are particularly troubling because we have witnessed a three-year increase in marijuana use among American teenagers, at a time when more potent forms of marijuana are readily available: Thirteen percent of eighth-graders reported having tried marijuana at least once in 1994—up from 9.2% in 1993, 7.2% in 1992, and 6.2% in 1991. Still, as we commit ourselves to countering this increase, we need to remember that there is also some important continuing good news. Adolescent marijuana use remains well below the levels of the late 1970s and early 1980s. This means that most young people do not use marijuana, and we need to remind them again and again of this crucial fact.

A HUGE MISTAKE

Given the facts, it is surprising that some people in Washington and elsewhere continue to bring up the issue of legalizing marijuana and other illicit drugs. That would be a huge mistake.

First, marijuana is a problem in our country because it is harmful—not because it is illicit. Research continues to show that it damages short-term memory, distorts perception, impairs judgment and complex motor skills, alters the heart rate, can lead to severe anxiety, and can cause paranoia and lethargy. Its use by young people is clearly associated with increased truancy, poor school performance and crime. And research by Roger Roffman and Robert Stephens at the University of Washington shows that marijuana can put a serious chokehold on long-term users who try to quit.

Second, marijuana use has great costs and consequences to all of us in society—not just to users. Young marijuana users are more likely than nonusers to use other illicit drugs, to have automobile crashes, and to be arrested. They are less likely to achieve their academic potential, which detracts from national productivity in the long run. They are at greater risk of needing expensive emergency room treatment, which costs us money in the short run. Indeed, in 1993, twice as many teenagers ended up in emergency rooms for marijuana use as for heroin and cocaine combined.

And, more broadly, drug use, including marijuana use, causes considerable damage in our workplaces. Few Americans realize that three-fourths of regular drug users are employed. According to the U.S. Chamber of Commerce, employed drug users are 33% less productive than their nonabusing colleagues. They are likely to incur 300% higher medical costs and benefits.

Third, legalization of marijuana almost certainly would cause more young people to use—and become addicted to—marijuana, as well as other drugs.

In part, that's because legalizing drugs takes away a significant deterrent against drug use. Moreover, for as long as we have monitored drug use, we have seen that whenever there is a decrease in the percentage of young people who perceive marijuana use as harmful, the percentage of users increases. Inevitably, legalization would suggest to young people that marijuana is not harmful—thereby knocking down a powerful barrier to use.

And even worse, because laws are rightly perceived by citizens in our democracy as the expression of national values, legalization would imply that marijuana use is an accepted—and acceptable—social practice. For many teenagers, that would intensify the already severe peer pressure they face to use drugs. Our daughters and sons would no longer have on their side the moral authority of our laws to bolster their antidrug attitudes and desire not to use drugs.

Indeed, reversing directions and legalizing marijuana could cause young people to dismiss warnings they have heard from government and the larger society about other illicit drugs like crack, cocaine and heroin—an erosion of trust that must never be allowed to happen.

What's behind the call for legalization of marijuana? Sometimes, it's a myth—like the false notion that marijuana is a "soft" drug. Sometimes it's the erroneous conclusion that legalization is the way to make drugs less prevalent in our country.

No Simple Solution

I believe there is a way to achieve a drug-free society—but there is no single, simple solution. The Clinton administration has embarked on a comprehensive drug strategy—a massive effort to reduce both the supply and the demand. In this effort, the role of the Department of Health and Human Services is critical: We are working with many partners to prevent drug use, provide effective treatment, conduct research on drug issues, and disseminate information to experts and the general public.

Specifically in relation to marijuana, we have taken a number of strong, targeted steps. We continue to fund major research on the effects of marijuana use on behavior. For example, . . . we expect publication of the results of a major, government-funded study showing the extent to which acute marijuana smoking and the potency of smoked marijuana are related to motivation to perform work tasks.

THE PROBLEMS OF LEGALIZATION

It is suggested that we legalize drugs, tax them, and use the vast windfall taxes to fund education and treatment to discourage drug use. Let's review our experience with legal drugs. We collect $12 billion in taxes annually from tobacco sales, and the estimated health costs associated with tobacco use are $75 billion a year. We collect $20 billion in taxes from alcohol sales, and the combined figure for alcohol-related health costs is $140 billion. How many of these bargains can we afford? How much would the government have to collect in taxes to offset the problems with wider drug use that would follow drug legalization? . . .

A recent national Gallup Poll revealed that 85% of Americans reject drug legalization. The public views the issue through the lens of common sense. It realizes that being under the influence of mind-altering substances is the problem, not the drug law.

Rachel Ehrenfeld, *Wall Street Journal*, February 7, 1996.

Based on our growing body of knowledge about marijuana, we have developed an aggressive communications strategy. For example, we know that it is critical to reach young people early, before they have begun to use drugs, with clear information about marijuana and with positive alternatives for their time. Young children typically have very strong antidrug attitudes; it's essential to reinforce them.

We also know that in order to stop marijuana use we must send young people clear and consistent messages. As a result, we are working across many media, with many partners, to tell young people: Don't start using marijuana, and if you have, stop right away. Marijuana use is illegal, dangerous and unhealthy. It is not cool. It is not respectful of one's body. And it is certainly not rampant among young people. This is a message we cannot emphasize enough.

Our research tells us something else as well. We know that young people need to hear antidrug messages where they live, where they study, where they work, where they play, and where they hang out. In other words, while the federal government must provide leadership, it cannot solve the drug problem alone—and it shouldn't try. We're recruiting parents and other family members to set drug-free examples for young people and talk with them about drugs. We're helping schools, community groups, religious organizations, the private sector, and state and local governments to join forces to give young people something to say "yes" to. We're meeting with the media and entertainment industries to promote programming that deglamorizes drug use and other risky behaviors. And we're challenging young people to work with us, knowing that teenagers have a unique gift for getting into each other's heads and influencing behavior.

A NATIONAL CHALLENGE

Make no mistake. We face a national challenge, and our young people are watching closely to see how we respond. We must not blink. . . . At a time when marijuana use has climbed, the foundation of success is education, prevention, treatment, research, law enforcement, interdiction and massive community involvement—not legalization or gutting our national commitment against drug use.

As we tighten our federal belts and rethink the scope and role of the federal government, we must never forget that the drug issue is about our national future. It is about real human beings, young people who have within them both a galaxy of gifts and a fragility that leaves them vulnerable to foolish choices and risky behavior. We must be there for them. We must do what is right for them and the nation.

"White supremacy and national oppression are woven into the very fabric of these drug laws."

FEDERAL DRUG LAWS ARE RACIST

Revolutionary Worker

In the following viewpoint, the Revolutionary Worker, a weekly newspaper published by the Revolutionary Communist Party, argues that U.S. federal drug policies are racist. The Revolutionary Worker contends that the government has targeted blacks for prosecution in crack cases; while most crack users are white, nearly 90 percent of people convicted on federal crack offenses are black. In addition, according to the Revolutionary Worker, the punishment for crack cocaine is more severe than that for powder cocaine, a policy that it says has resulted in the imprisonment of a disproportionate number of blacks.

As you read, consider the following questions:

1. What evidence does the Revolutionary Worker give to show that America's criminal justice system in general is racist?
2. How does the Revolutionary Worker refute the government's argument that crack causes more social harm than does cocaine?
3. What is the primary difference between crack and powder cocaine, according to the Revolutionary Worker?

"Supreme Court Upholds Racist Crack Laws," Revolutionary Worker, May 26, 1996. Reprinted by permission of RCP Publications, Chicago. Greenhaven Press has changed the title of this article and added the graph.

In a near-unanimous decision, the highest court in the country ruled in favor of racist government policies on crack prosecutions. The May 13, 1996, ruling by the U.S. Supreme Court overturned rulings by the Ninth Circuit Court of Appeals in San Francisco and a district court in L.A. which dismissed federal charges against five men accused of selling crack. The dismissal came after the government prosecutors refused to obey the judge's order to explain statistics showing a clear disparity in the number of Black and white people who are prosecuted for federal crack offenses.

The statistics are shocking. The majority of crack users are white, according to the government's own figures. But a study of the 1993 convictions showed that 88.3 percent of those convicted on federal crack offenses were Black, 7.1 percent Latino and 4.1 percent white. In the original case involving the five men accused of selling crack, the defense had presented an affidavit from the federal public defender's office in L.A. showing that the defendants in all 24 crack cocaine cases brought to conclusion by the office in 1991 were African American. In the federal courts of 16 states, not a single white person was tried for crack offenses between 1987 and 1992.

These numbers clearly point to the racist targeting of Black people by the government in crack cases. Yet the Supreme Court justices ruled that these statistics by themselves were not a "credible showing" of racist prosecution practices.

RACIST SENTENCING GUIDELINES

Along with the stark disparity in prosecution rates, there is also the racist nature of sentencing guidelines for drug-related offenses. The mandatory sentencing guidelines passed by the Congress distinguish between crack and powder cocaine. This distinction has led to a huge disproportion in arrests, convictions and sentencing of young Black males for felony drug offenses.

Under these guidelines people convicted on federal charges for five grams of crack are punished with a mandatory minimum sentence of five years without parole, even for first-time offenders. By contrast, a mandatory minimum of five years for powdered cocaine kicks in at possession of 500 grams—100 times the amount of crack.

According to estimates by the federal Sentencing Commission, 14,000 out of 90,000 federal prison inmates are serving sentences under these laws for crack cocaine offenses.

As mentioned earlier, almost 90 percent of those convicted on federal crack offenses in 1993 were Black. Those convicted of powdered cocaine in that same year were 32 percent white, 27.4 percent Black and 39.3 percent Latino.

The racist federal guidelines on crack interpenetrate with more general discrimination against Black people in the justice system—contributing to a situation where today one in three Black men between the ages of 20 and 29 are in prison or on probation.

INDIVIDUALS CONVICTED ON FEDERAL CRACK OFFENSES, BY RACE, IN 1993

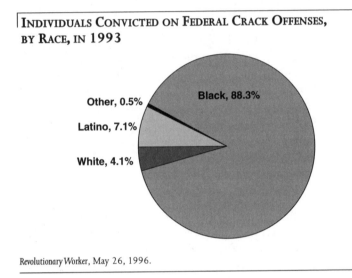

Other, 0.5%

Latino, 7.1%

White, 4.1%

Black, 88.3%

Revolutionary Worker, May 26, 1996.

About 13 percent of monthly drug users are Black. But Black people make up 35 percent of arrests for drug possession; 55 percent of all convictions for drug possession and 74 percent of all prison sentences for drug possession. As of 1992 the incarceration rates among Black males were eight times higher than white males.

THE GOVERNMENT'S BOGUS ARGUMENTS

The government bases the discriminatory drug laws on the argument that crack wreaks greater social damages than powder cocaine. They claim that crack use is "more associated with gang violence." They say that crack is more dangerous because it is more potent, addictive and affordable.

But defense attorneys and others who have studied the issue contradict the government's argument about crack's "association with violence." One public defender said: "We see street-level guys all the time who sell $20 doses [of crack]. They end up in federal court facing a massive amount of time. They don't have gang affiliations. They don't have firearms. They shouldn't be there."

Medical experts point out that there are negligible pharmacological differences between crack and powdered cocaine. Though smoking crack makes the drug's high quicker and stronger, some doctors note that powdered cocaine when free-based can also be smoked or injected, which is more likely to lead to addiction.

When Congress first passed the mandatory sentencing laws, there was much talk of busting "drug kingpins." This argument was bogus even on its own terms. Since crack cocaine must be made from powder, those who handle powder cocaine are higher up on the drug "food chain." Crack is also sold in small quantities at lower prices than powder—so higher penalties for "affordability" only penalizes the poor. The result is that most of those in federal court are street-level offenders. A 1993 survey by a government commission could only find eight high-level dealers out of 146 cases. And there is evidence that the feds actually go out of their way to bust small dealers, using the practice of "bargaining up." This involves sending agents back to a small dealer repeatedly until the total reaches the 50 grams necessary to kick in a 10-year sentence.

When the myths are stripped away, the primary difference between crack and powder is the public perception of the user and the seller—the white suburbanite is usually linked with powdered cocaine and the young urban Black man connected to crack. And it has been in the interests of the power structure to perpetuate this public image—in order to justify harsh police controls over poor and volatile oppressed communities. The reality is that white supremacy and national oppression are woven into the very fabric of these drug laws.

THE SYSTEM DEFENDS ITS RACIST LAWS

The statistics on the disparity in crack laws are so blatant that in 1995, even the official U.S. Sentencing Commission was moved to act. The Sentencing Commission, established by Congress to set uniform sentencing guidelines for federal courts, recommended that the distinction between crack and powder be eliminated and that the punishment for crack be reduced to that for powder.

"Federal sentencing data leads to the inescapable conclusion that blacks comprise the largest percentage of those affected by the penalties associated with crack cocaine," said the commission.

Thousands of families with young men serving long sentences for drug convictions were hopeful that the recommendation by the Sentencing Commission would bring some changes in the law. But both the Senate and the House vetoed the recommendation and voted to keep the current sentencing guidelines. It was the first of 500 recommendations made by the commission to be rejected since its creation in 1984.

It was not only the Republican-dominated Congress that threw out the recommendation—the Clinton administration also rejected it.

Federal courts have consistently rejected the argument that the 100-to-1 ratio between crack and powder cocaine violates the equal protection clause of the Constitution. And now, the Supreme Court has contributed its official stamp of approval.

These moves by the courts, the Congress and the presidency show that the highest levels of the power structure think it is in the interests of their system to maintain and enforce the racist drug laws.

> "The vast majority of prosecutors, police officers, and legislators base their decisions not on 'racial animus' but on the realities of the crack epidemic."

FEDERAL DRUG LAWS ARE NOT RACIST

Cristopher Rapp

Federal laws against the possession and sale of crack cocaine are more severe than those for powder cocaine. Some commentators argue that this disparity is racist because it results in the prosecution and imprisonment of large numbers of blacks. In the following viewpoint, Cristopher Rapp insists that the severity of the laws against crack does not result from racial discrimination but from the fact that crack is a much more destructive drug than powder cocaine. Rapp is an investigative journalism project fellow with the Center for the Study of Popular Culture, a conservative think tank.

As you read, consider the following questions:
1. What guidelines do prosecutors use when deciding whether to charge a suspect with a federal drug crime, according to Rapp?
2. According to Bryan A. Liang, quoted by the author, why is it appropriate for law enforcement officials to target urban communities?
3. What does Rapp mean when he says that failing to severely punish crack users and dealers would be racist?

Excerpted from "Slipping Through the Crack," Heterodoxy, vol. 4, no. 3 (March 1996); © Heterodoxy magazine. Reprinted by permission of the editors.

The argument . . . that federal prosecution and sentencing for crack unfairly and unconstitutionally target black defendants is based on two related, but separate issues—the disparity in the percentages of black and white defendants prosecuted in federal court; and the disparity between the amount of crack and the amount of powder cocaine required to trigger federal mandatory minimum sentences. . . .

A considerable majority of federal crack cases do in fact involve black defendants. For example, from January 1, 1991, through March 31, 1995, 75% (109 out of 146) of the defendants prosecuted in federal court for crack in the Central District of California were black, while during the same period only one white defendant was prosecuted.

Nationally in 1994, . . . blacks comprised roughly 90% of the 3,600 federal crack defendants; whites made up 3.5%. Critics charge that this "disparate impact" indicates that prosecutors engage in selective prosecution. Not only this, but on average, a defendant convicted in federal court for drug offenses receives a sentence of 86 months for trafficking and 22 months for possession, compared to 36 months and 12 months in the state system. More significantly, say critics of the present system, federal law itself dictates harsher penalties for crack, the form often associated with the black community, than for powder cocaine, the form associated with more affluent white users, by a ratio of close to 100 to 1.

TRUE CHARGES?

This 100-1 ratio has caused the brunt of the criticism from academics, politicians, and the popular press. For example, Jesse Jackson has called the statutes "a moral disgrace," which condemns "thousands of young African American and Latino men to languish unjustly in prison." Berkeley Law Professor Jerome Skolnick described the ratio as "absurd, foolish and outrageous," and suggested that Congress would be displaying a "racial animus" if it did not amend the law. A *Los Angeles Times* editorial referred to the sentences for crack as "Draconian punishment," and Knoll Lowney, a professor of law at Washington University, wrote that the ratio results in the "overincarceration" of black males, and held it responsible for most of the ills of the black community. A special report of the U.S. Sentencing Commission released in May of 1995 shared these sentiments, recommending that the penalties for crack and powder be made equal.

As these charges attain the status of received truth, their potential implications become clear. At best, they suggest that an underlying racism taints the country's war on drugs; at worst they point to a racist government conspiracy of (Johnnie) Cochran–esque proportions. But a closer analysis of the prosecution data and of the differences in the impact of crack and powder cocaine suggests that the vast majority of prosecutors, police officers, and legislators base their decisions not on "racial animus" but on the realities of the crack epidemic and those most affected by it.

ABSURD CRITICISM

Critics of the federal government's war on illegal narcotics trafficking have seized on a new angle: reckless allegations of racism. . . . These critics conclude that African Americans are being prosecuted in federal court solely because of their race. . . .

What nonsense. The U.S. attorney's office prosecutes only those whose crimes are serious enough to meet the office's high thresholds for drug quantity and aggravating factors—thresholds designed to ensure that scarce federal resources are spent where they will have the greatest impact. . . .

The federal government focuses its limited resources on communities whose residents have suffered the most from the destructive impact of crack. Those residents are largely African American, as are the criminals who terrorize them. That's why most crack traffickers in federal court are African Americans.

Nora M. Manella, *Los Angeles Times*, June 13, 1995.

The critics of the federal policy base their claims solely on the fact that a large majority of federal crack prosecutions—75% in the Central District of California and 90% nationally—involve black defendants. Since blacks make up such a high percentage of federal crack prosecutions, they argue, federal prosecutors must be taking race into account when they choose whom to try in federal court, and whom to leave to the state courts. In other words, at least one of the following must be true: 1) the criteria used to select defendants for federal prosecution must discriminate according to race; otherwise, 2) officials must apply guidelines in a racially discriminatory way, having one set of standards for blacks and another for whites.

In fact, the actual guidelines used by the U.S. Attorney's Office in the Central District show that decisions regarding prosecution are neither capricious nor discriminatory. The first guideline concerns the total quantity of crack possessed or distributed by the defendant. The average federal defendant has sold 109 grams of crack, and the overwhelming majority have sold at least 50 grams. Other factors which heavily influence prosecutors' decisions include the defendant's prior felony record and his use or possession of a firearm in connection with the crack offense. Membership in a violent street gang or criminal organization, while not sufficient to qualify a defendant for federal prosecution, can also be considered; this factor has particular importance in Los Angeles, where the sale of crack remains in large measure the province of violent gangs. Finally, cases only become eligible for federal prosecution in the first place when federal agencies play a part of the investigation and/or arrest, or when state officials bring the case to the U.S. Attorney's attention.

These guidelines hardly form the basis of selective prosecution. (All people regardless of race, obviously enough, are equally capable of not getting involved with the sale of crack.) In theory, of course, even clearly race-neutral guidelines such as these can be applied in a racially discriminatory manner. But a case by case analysis of the federal crack indictments in the Central District between January 1, 1992, and March 31, 1995, suggests that race does not play any role in prosecutorial decisions. Of the 146 defendants charged during this period 94.3% either met the quantity requirements, employed firearms, or had prior drug records. All of the cases filed in 1992, 1993, and 1995 qualified for federal prosecution under the quantity guidelines alone. The remaining cases—eight—involved other aggravating factors such as gang involvement and prior violent felony record.

NO EVIDENCE

After looking at these statistics, . . . U.S. District Judge Dickran Tevrizian decided that the claims were unfounded: "There is no evidence that the charging decision in any of the cocaine base [i.e. crack] cases . . . was based upon the defendant's race, ethnic origins, or gender, or upon any other impermissible factor."

The same holds true nationwide. Professor John J. DiIulio, of Princeton's Woodrow Wilson School and the Brookings Institute, cites a 1993 study of federal drug sentencing from 1986–1990 in concluding that crack cocaine sentencing statutes did not result in racially discriminatory sentences. "The amount of the drug sold," DiIulio wrote, "the offenders' prior criminal records, whether weapons were involved, and other characteristics that federal law and sentencing guidelines established as valid considerations accounted for all the observed variation in sentencing."

If the charges against the U.S. Attorney's Office were true—if "disparate impact" were proof of selective prosecution—one would expect that the state courts would be full of white crack offenders who were passed over for federal prosecution by the racially biased prosecutors. The facts do not bear this out. A study of federal and state crack defendants between January 1, 1990, and August 11, 1992, shows no evidence that prosecutors allowed whites eligible for federal prosecution to remain in the state courts. . . .

Despite the elaborate conspiracy theories of critics of national drug policy, statistical and anecdotal evidence suggest that federal crack prosecution figures result from the real-world demographics of crack rather than racial discrimination. Few people would dispute the idea that blacks make up a large percentage of crack abusers. Even fewer would disagree that crack has wreaked its worst havoc in the black community. As the *Los Angeles Times* reported in a 1994 series on the crack epidemic, "for a variety of social reasons, the drug has burned its greatest swath through low-income, mostly minority neighborhoods, where for only $5 or $10 it offers in concentrated form a high [otherwise] available only to those who could afford costly powder cocaine.". . .

No one accuses crack of being an equal-opportunity destroyer. Like the street gangs which make their living selling it, crack has worked its way into—and does its most damage in—low income urban black communities, where its influence is abetted by other social pathologies. Given this situation, says Professor Bryan A. Liang of Pepperdine Law School, it makes sense that prosecutors and law enforcement officials should focus their attention in dealing with crack in at risk communities. Liang characterizes the decision as an economic rather than a racial one:

> In a world like ours in which you have limited resources, you have to go into the communities which are most affected by the criminal activity. For crack that would be the urban communities. . . . So you have to go there. You have to go where the crime is. You can't pick and choose on the basis of race where to prosecute in order to be "fair." You have to use your resources to get rid of the most crime possible. . . .

A QUICK HIGH

Those who defend the 100-1 ratio argue that the comparison between crack and cocaine is chemically as well as legally justified. Because of crack's high concentration and the fact that it is smoked rather than snorted it tends to be much more addictive than powder. Crack reaches the brain sixteen times faster than powder—in about 19 seconds—and the drug takes its effect in one-twentieth the time. The resulting high is both more intense and shorter lasting than a powder—a high which translates into more frequent bingeing, and a quicker psychological addiction.

Retired Circuit Court Judge Edward Rogers says this feature makes crack particularly dangerous. "I know a lot of people who did powder cocaine socially at parties, or once a month, or once every three months, or every now and then, and they could take it or leave it," he says. "I don't know many people who have experimented like that with crack. The crack dealers will give you stuff [for free] to get you hooked. It is just so addictive.". . .

CRACK AND VIOLENCE

Crack's increasingly close association with violence also seems to set it apart from traditional cocaine. Drug-related violent crime increased all over the country when crack hit the scene, with murder rates going up in some cities by 50%. The U.S. Sentencing Commission makes note of this unique aspect of the crack epidemic when it says that "crack dealers generally tend to have a stronger association with systemic violence [violence associated with the marketing of a drug] and are more likely to possess weapons than powder cocaine dealers."

In addition to increasing the level of violence in the community, says Los Angeles Sheriff Sherman Block, "we saw a whole new kind of violence. Not only did the incidence of violence go up, the nature of the violence changed in that we were witnessing more random violence, violence seemingly for the sake of violence."

The close relationship between crack and violent crime exacts other social costs as well. The health care costs associated with crack use astound. The number of cocaine-related medical emergencies in the US has increased 500% since 1983, with crack largely responsible for the rise. The high potency of the drug causes some users to suffer severe internal organ damage. Treatment for drug-exposed infants, the vast majority of whom had been exposed to crack, cost L.A. County public hospitals approximately $22 million in 1991 alone. An individual case of crack exposure—there are over 2,000 in the county each year—can cost anywhere from $8,000 to over $200,000 per child.

The desperate addiction associated with the drug has made "strawberries"—prostitutes who work for crack—fixtures of the crack culture. According to one estimate the AIDS rate in crack-infested areas can reach as high as one in five. Crack has also made a major contribution to homelessness in the nation's cities. In some locations estimates indicate that as much as 80% of the local homeless population uses crack.

SOCIETY'S NIGHTMARE

Low prices help fuel the boom and make crack's intense high— and quick addiction—available to just about anyone. Sold in doses as small as one-tenth of a gram, crack can be had for as little as two dollars. Michael Reed, a drug abuse counselor at Southern California Alcohol and Drug Programs, Inc., says that the drug's low cost explains its high concentration in low-income neighborhoods. "It's an addict's dream and a society's nightmare," he says, "a cheap high. It's extremely addictive and extremely inexpensive, which takes it right into poor areas and keeps it there."

Even the youngest members of those communities can afford a rock which costs less than a McDonald's Happy Meal. Reed goes so far as to say that "crack was designed for a school-aged child. A child can save his lunch money and by Friday have enough money to get loaded all weekend."

Powder cocaine, to be sure, takes a heavy toll on its users, but it does not seem to have the devastating, communitywide impact which crack does. Walter Williams, the black Chairman of Economics at George Mason University, remarks that "people out in the suburbs using powder cocaine don't see the kind of stuff going on that you see in the inner cities with the use of crack."

Powder cocaine's higher price, lower potency, and lesser addictive qualities may explain this. In addition, suggests Professor Liang, the demographics of those who use two drugs magnify the differences between crack and cocaine.

A drug of the middle and upper classes, "powder cocaine definitely has an effect on those individuals, but they have social structures that they can fall back upon. They have more stable family lives, they aren't as desperate. . . . The people who use crack are so close to the edge [in economic and social terms] that crack just pushes them over."

In the words of Sister Alice Callaghan, director of the Las Familias del Pueblo family service agency in Los Angeles, "When you are disadvantaged and you throw crack into that, you absolutely can't make it. . . . Crack just crumbles you. It pins you to the ground."

Given crack's effects on both the user and the surrounding community and the fact that it is pandemic in the black ghetto, it would seem to be racist NOT to punish its sale more severely than other drugs.

| "Colombia is no longer a reliable ally
in the U.S. war on drugs."

THE U.S. SHOULD PRESSURE COLOMBIA TO STRENGTHEN ITS ANTIDRUG EFFORTS

John P. Sweeney

Colombia is one of the world's leading producers of illegal drugs. In the following viewpoint, John P. Sweeney argues that the illegal drug trade has adversely affected the Colombian government and economy, threatening the security of Latin America as well as the United States. Sweeney, who is a policy analyst at the Heritage Foundation, a conservative think tank in Washington, D.C., recommends several measures designed to pressure the Colombian government to increase its efforts to combat drug production and trafficking.

As you read, consider the following questions:

1. What seven measures does Sweeney believe would improve Colombia's antidrug record?
2. What evidence does the author give to support his view that the Colombian government and business sectors benefit from drug trafficking?
3. Sweeney suggests that the United States "isolate Colombia internationally." How could this be done, in his opinion?

Excerpted from "Colombia's Narco-Democracy Threatens Hemispheric Security" by John P. Sweeney, *Backgrounder*, March 21, 1995. Copyright 1995 by The Heritage Foundation. Reprinted by permission of The Heritage Foundation.

For the first time since 1986, when the U.S. started passing judgment on the counternarcotics efforts of 29 major drug-producing and drug-transit countries, Colombia in 1995 received a failing grade. However, President Clinton issued a "national interest waiver" exempting it from this failing grade. As a result, Colombia will be eligible for continued U.S. aid even though it is not doing enough to stop the illegal drug trade.

This policy is deeply misguided. The threat to U.S. and hemispheric security posed by Colombia's narco-democracy cannot be overestimated. The U.S. may be the world's largest consumer of drugs, but Colombia ranks third in the world in per capita consumption. Literally every country in the Americas has a serious domestic drug crisis. The drug cartels are well-positioned to influence Latin America's economic reforms and manipulate the region's weak political and judicial institutions. In Colombia, they have penetrated the regulatory and lawmaking processes to the point that they can influence constitutional and financial reform. They also have been financing election campaigns for many years, and at least three Colombian presidents have knowingly taken money from drug traffickers.

WHAT THE U.S. SHOULD DO

Congress should demand an explanation from the Clinton Administration. Why should the U.S. provide aid to stop the drug trade and support Colombia's economic development when Colombia's government is not serious about ending the production and trafficking of narcotics? The Clinton Administration's counternarcotics policy clearly is not working. It should be reviewed with two objectives in mind: to establish tougher standards for Colombia and to increase pressure on the Colombian government to eradicate the drug cartels. Specifically, the U.S. should:

• *Decertify Colombia for its lack of cooperation with the U.S.* Decertification would block Colombia's access to financial and technical aid from the multilateral development banks and should trigger the suspension of all counternarcotics aid to Colombia as well. The U.S. should not consider granting even a "national interest" recertification until President Ernesto Samper dispels, with actions instead of words, international perceptions that he has been compromised by the Cali cartel.

• *Insist that Colombia sign an extradition treaty with the U.S.* This would allow Colombian citizens under indictment in the U.S. for drug trafficking, money laundering, and other drug-related crimes to be extradited to the U.S.

• *Urge Colombia to sign a bilateral law enforcement treaty with the U.S.*

Colombia would agree to enact tough money-laundering and sentencing laws for narcotics traffickers and to confiscate all commercial, real estate, and personal assets owned by convicted traffickers.

• *Develop specific performance benchmarks for Colombia as a condition for any renewed bilateral assistance.*

• *Hold extensive congressional hearings to review Colombia's counter-drug cooperation and performance.* These hearings should focus on narco-politics and narco-corruption in both Colombia and Mexico, since drug cartels in both countries are working together to flood the United States with drugs and weapons.

• *Impose visa prohibitions on Colombian officials, regardless of rank, who are implicated in narco-corruption or any drug-related offenses.*

• *End Colombia's participation in the Andean Trade Preferences Act (ATPA).* This would mean that Colombian products would lose preferential tariff access to U.S. markets, potentially costing the Colombian economy hundreds of millions of dollars in reduced export earnings.

THE WORLD'S FIRST NARCO-DEMOCRACY

U.S. counternarcotics experts believe that Colombia is the world's first narco-democracy, a country whose economy, political system, and society have been profoundly compromised and distorted by the wealth and power of the drug cartels. Former President Misael Pastrana, who governed Colombia from 1974–1978, asserts: "El Tiempo [Bogota's leading daily newspaper] talks about a 'narco-project.' People talk about 'narco-crimes,' they talk about 'narco-money,' and if you add that up, logically it implies general contamination."

Joe Toft, former head of the U.S. Drug Enforcement Agency (DEA) in Bogota, claims that Colombia is "already at the abyss." Narco-democracy "really is here [in Colombia]," he said during a live interview with Colombian television. "I can't think of a single institution in Colombia that I know of, with any judicial, legal or political influence, which does not have problems of penetration by the narcotics traffickers. The Attorney General's office has serious problems. Congress is also very infiltrated by narco-traffickers. . . . Everything favors [the] Cali [drug cartel]. They got rid of extradition, which was the only thing they truly feared. And now the situation is very favorable [for the drug kingpins]."

Colombian drug traffickers repatriate between $3 billion and $7 billion a year in laundered drug-related earnings from the United States and Europe, according to U.S. counter-drug analyst. Drug money has created a construction frenzy in Colombia's main cities—Bogota, Medellin, Cali, and Barranquilla—and has pushed up the prices of land and housing drastically. In a country where the minimum wage is 31 cents an hour, four-bedroom apartments are selling for up to $400,000 in cash. U.S. and government authorities have evidence that drug proceeds have been deposited in every major bank in Colombia.

Every resident of Cali or Medellin is affected directly or indirectly by drug-tainted money. For example, a $10 million deposit of drug money in a Cali or Medellin bank may be loaned out to build a new apartment complex. This money eventually trickles down to the local economy for the purchase of everyday goods and services. Drug trafficking proceeds have been a primary source of revenue for the cities of Cali and Medellin since the mid-1980s, and more recently for Barranquilla, according to U.S. anti-drug analysts.

BRIBING THE GOVERNMENT

U.S. officials complain that Bogota has not aggressively pursued the Cali drug lords, and the State Department has criticized the government of President Ernesto Samper for "weak legislation, corruption and inefficiency.". . .

Accusations persist that Colombia lacks the will to get tough because of the cartel's bribes to government officials, which allegedly include a $3.2 million campaign contribution to President Samper.

Linda Robinson, U.S. News & World Report, June 19, 1995.

The DEA believes that "the revenue generated by the influx of drug proceeds into the economy has provided the Colombian Government with funds for debt payments and national infrastructure development. . . . [T]hrough the purchase of government-issued securities, Colombian drug kingpins are investing in their country's future development. The immense resources of the drug cartels afford them a cushion of security in Colombia. Their influence within the banking industry, government, and law enforcement agencies already has impeded attempts to prosecute them. Through bribery and intimidation, they have altered and reversed undesired policy decisions by the country's government and banking regulators."

The Colombian drug cartels have expanded their operations around the world significantly since the early 1990s. U.S. counternarcotics intelligence agencies have identified at least 14 "core" Colombian cartels in business with 19 Mexican cartels to transport Colombian-produced cocaine and heroin into the United States. Since the 1980s, the Colombian cartels have opened new consumer markets for cocaine in practically every Latin American country. Venezuela has become a major drug-transit country; Panama retains its historical position as a key drug-transit and money-laundering country; and Guatemala has emerged as an important "warehousing" country, used by Colombian and Mexican cartels running loosely integrated drug trafficking operations.

In Europe, the Colombian drug barons are doing business with the Sicilian Mafia and other criminal groups in Italy, Germany, France, and Britain. They also are penetrating Eastern Europe and opening new markets in Russia in association with Russia's thriving criminal underworld. Although the production and international distribution of cocaine and heroin is their primary business, Colombian cartels also trade in weapons, icons, raw materials, radioactive materials, and counterfeit U.S. dollars.

THE OFFICIAL POSITION

The Colombian government and many Colombians express outrage at the word "narco-democracy," rejecting the argument that drug cartels have thoroughly penetrated every aspect of Colombian society. The official government line on the Colombian drug problem is that the drug traffickers comprise a very small minority and that Colombians have battled the drug traffickers much longer, and have died in far greater numbers, than anyone else. The drug problem is described by the Colombian government as an international issue that requires international solutions.

But Colombians tend to overlook the global reach and power of their country's drug cartels. Colombia's five-year-old constitution bans the extradition of Colombian citizens wanted for crimes committed in other countries, and the courts rarely punish drug traffickers. In fact, 38 percent of the drug traffickers who turn themselves in through the plea bargain system never spend a single day in jail. . . .

The Samper Administration's response to President Clinton's decision to downgrade Colombia with a "national interest" certification was a mixture of rejection and defiance. Officials close to Samper suggested that Colombia might choose to reject all future U.S. assistance in the counternarcotics war rather than subject their country to a review by the U.S. government which many Colombians consider to be both unfair and biased against them.

The Samper Administration's view was summed up in its official response to the DEA's report on the impact of money laundering in the Colombian economy. In this document, the Samper government defended Colombia's financial controls as adequate, denied that drug traffickers have a significant impact on the Colombian economy, and charged that the DEA is opposed to a free-market economy with a strong and vigorous private sector: "The document circulated by the DEA shows profound ignorance on how the Colombian economy operates. . . . Due to its lack of methodology or scientific accuracy and to its bias against the country, the [DEA] document constitutes not only an insult to Colombians, but an insult to intelligence."

PRESSURING COLOMBIA

The Clinton Administration's current counternarcotics policy is not working in the case of Colombia. Something must be done to stem the flow of drugs from the world's most powerful cocaine cartels. The U.S. should consider every possible avenue for compelling the Colombian government to crack down on these criminal cartels. . . .

By any standard, Colombia is no longer a reliable ally in the U.S. war on drugs. The time has come to begin treating the Colombian government as part of the American drug problem rather than part of the solution. Recognizing this with presidential decertification is an important first step. This will help to prevent Colombia from obtaining assistance from multilateral financial institutions, which in effect are helping to subsidize the production of Colombia's poisonous narcotics exports.

Beyond this, the U.S. should take the lead in isolating Colombia internationally. This will involve denying visas to known drug operatives in the Colombian government and even withdrawing trade preferences for Colombian exports as permitted by the Andean Trade Preferences Act (ATPA). While trade is a blunt and usually inappropriate tool for governments, in this case it will send the clear signal that Colombia no longer deserves the preferential treatment provided by the ATPA.

Finally, the Clinton Administration must reaffirm its commitment to the war on drugs, which had begun to show substantial progress by 1992. Unfortunately, most of the earlier gains have been reversed because of President Clinton's benign neglect of the problem. Colombia's national interest recertification is only the most recent example of this. Although much ridiculed as an insufficient response at the time, the Reagan Administration's "Just Say No" effort was more successful than many want to admit. It is time to just say no to Colombia.

"For Colombia, fighting drugs is both
a national security issue and a
moral obligation."

COLOMBIA IS ALREADY COMMITTED
TO FIGHTING DRUGS

Ernesto Samper

Ernesto Samper is the president of Colombia. In the following
viewpoint, Samper defends his nation's record in fighting the
production and trafficking of illegal drugs. He insists that
Colombia has improved its ability to track down and arrest drug
lords and has destroyed thousands of acres of drug crops. Samper suggests that other nations, including the United States,
should work to increase international cooperation in efforts to
combat the illegal drug trade.

As you read, consider the following questions:
1. What specific measures has Colombia taken to decrease the
   production of drugs in that country, according to Samper?
2. What five measures does Samper believe would improve
   international cooperation in the fight against drugs?
3. What are precursor chemicals? What must nations do to
   control them, in the author's view?

The world's attention was riveted in June 1995 by pictures of the most dangerous drug lord in the world being brought to justice by elite units of the Colombian government. By all accounts, the arrest of Gilberto Rodriguez Orejuela, leader of the Cali cartel, is a devastating blow against the scourge of narcotics and organized crime. Where should the worldwide fight against drugs go from here?

My administration's policy has been to launch an integrated, multifront attack on the cartels. That is why, since January 1995, the government and the office of the prosecutor general have targeted the cartels' bank accounts, laboratories, crops, chemicals, transportation systems and political connections. With the help of global allies, we created a system of improved law enforcement, better intelligence to penetrate trafficker's communications, aggressive crop eradication, accelerated detection and destruction of labs and precursor chemicals, and sophisticated measures to track money-laundering.

This integrated policy may have been a more deliberate, long-term approach than some would have liked. In the past, the focus has been on disrupting the drug trade. My integrated policy is intended to dismantle the many components of the cartels' operations. With the capture of Rodriguez Orejuela, those who questioned whether Colombia was fully committed to the fight have been proved wrong.

THE DEATHS OF INNOCENTS

Though we are aware that this arrest may unleash a wave of renewed violence in our country, we will persevere. In the past decade, Colombia has lost countless lives, including more than 3,000 police officers and soldiers, 23 judges, 63 journalists and four presidential candidates. Hundreds of innocent civilians have been killed—33 in Medellin from a drug-inspired bomb blast two days after Rodriguez Orejuela's capture.

Colombia has been under enormous pressure from our allies to step up our attacks against the cartels. We understand why our friends have asked this of us. But let us be clear: We have hunted these criminals and will continue to do so because, for Colombia, fighting drugs is both a national security issue and a moral obligation. Between January and June 1995:
- Cartel bank accounts have been put in danger by a historic law against money-laundering.
- About 25,000 acres of coca crops and over 5,400 acres of heroin crops have been eradicated, much more than were destroyed in all of 1994.

- More than 440,000 gallons of cartel liquid chemicals and 3.8 million kilos of solid chemical used to process drugs have been seized.
- 64,277 grams of heroin have been taken.
- 243 drug labs have been destroyed.
- Colombia's offshore Caribbean islands have been militarized to interrupt drug transport and air delivery systems.
- The city of Cali, with a population of more than two million people, has been the target of an unprecedented police crackdown to disrupt drug operations and communications.

The results speak for themselves. Rodriguez Orejuela was the 1,118th cartel criminal arrested [in 1995]. This is the beginning of the end of the Cali cartel.

The arrest of Rodriguez Orejuela gives the world a chance to ponder the next steps in the fight against narcotics and crime. Aside from isolated successes, the world's 15-year fight against drugs has, at best, been a stalemate. While international crime organizations are modernizing their operations and coordinating their activities, international cooperation remains undeveloped. Any new international strategy must involve every country affected by drugs and target each stage of the drug trade, including cultivation, production, transportation, distribution, consumption and money-laundering.

A GLOBAL STRATEGY IS NEEDED

In the same fashion that Colombia is beginning to show results with a domestic integrated strategy, we must adopt a global integrated strategy. If we don't, the battle Colombia has been waging may be lost at the global level.

Unfortunately, drug use is reported up in all European capitals and is expanding into new markets in Eastern Europe and Asia. In the U.S., the largest narcotics consumer among industrialized nations, cocaine-related emergencies (considered a reliable measure of drug use) are up 25% since 1991 and heroin use is rising sharply. Colombia defeated the Medellin cartel in the 1980s and is determined to do the same in Cali. But there will always be more cartels around the world to supply drugs as long as there is the demand.

Let us move beyond the traditional definitions of supply vs. demand, or consumption vs. production. The lessons of the past have proved that more is needed. A policy of heightened international cooperation would require decisive actions on a number of fronts. I offer the following initial recommendations:

- *Create a forum for heightened judicial cooperation.* Sharing evidence, intelligence and information to speed up investigations and prosecutions of drug cases is increasingly important. Such cooperation would force a regular follow-up on ideas of mutual concern to countries.

• *Accelerate work on an inter-American treaty against money-laundering.* The global narcotics trade is valued at about $500 billion a year, 75% of which is laundered through the world's leading financial markets. The only way to thwart the laundering is to ensure that banking and financial laws are harmonized throughout the hemisphere.

• *Discuss stricter controls on the trade of precursor chemicals.* While chemicals such as ether, acetone and sulfuric acid are legitimate substances used in many industries, they are essential for making heroin and cocaine. Countries allied in the war against drugs need to track these chemicals—much as they track pharmaceuticals and financial instruments—without hindering legitimate companies producing these substances.

• *Involve the multilateral system in serious crop-substitution efforts.* In Colombia, we have eradicated thousands of acres of coca and poppy and have put in place a crop-substitution program. The world's finance ministers should discuss how the World Bank, the Inter-American Development Bank and the Asian Development Bank could propel such national programs to more effective levels.

• *Call a World Summit on Drugs, as suggested by Mexican President Ernesto Zedillo.* Narcotics and the crime and corruption they cause are a critical global issue. A world conference could become a catalyst to harmonize policies and laws against narcotics to make our fight more effective. In 1992, there was a Global Summit on the Environment; in 1995, there was a Summit on Social Development, and a Summit on Women. Certainly narcotics is just as important an issue.

The world needs to adopt a comprehensive international drug eradication and enforcement strategy. At times, Colombia has felt alone in this fight. With increased international cooperation, we will succeed against the traffickers. In the interim, no one should doubt Colombia's commitment to do all we can in the international effort against drugs.

"What Holland could teach a more
moralistic America is: Figure out
what you can reasonably expect to
do . . . and . . . plan so that you
diminish the problem."

THE U.S. SHOULD COPY HOLLAND'S DRUG POLICIES

Georgie Anne Geyer

Holland treats drug abuse as a public health problem, not as a
legal or moral problem, Georgie Anne Geyer explains in the following viewpoint. While most drugs are still illegal, users are
rarely punished. Instead, the Dutch focus on treating hard-core
addicts and punishing users for antisocial behavior, not for drug
use itself. Geyer argues that these policies are sensible and effective, and they should be adopted by the U.S. government. Geyer
is a nationally syndicated columnist.

As you read, consider the following questions:

1. According to Geyer, how does the Dutch policy achieve social
   peace?
2. How have Dutch policies affected the number of young hard-
   core drug users, according to the author?
3. How did a Dutch mayor's willingness to legalize heroin affect
   heroin addicts, according to Geyer?

Heroin is illegal in Amsterdam, but even pushers may not get "busted" if they are (1) quiet or (2) do not offend sensibilities by getting too rich from drugs. Marijuana is also illegal, but virtually nobody ever gets in trouble for smoking it publicly.

As a matter of fact, prostitution is also illegal in Holland, but along the canals in the "red light" area, nearly naked women painted up like the baddest of the bad actually sit in the windows—and they are not getting ready to swim!

"You see we manage all of this," said Ernst Bruning, director of the international affairs bureau of the Municipal Health Service, as he talked to me about the different morality here. "We try in Holland to manage social problems. It's a different paradigm."

Indeed, to understand the Netherlands' managed social morality—and in particular, their unique drug program—I have come back here on a regular basis (and beautiful Amsterdam makes it easy). The last time I visited—in 1989—I made a list of the words and phrases they use: "harm reduction," "non-moralistic judgments," "a Junkie Union," "no shame," "no crack," "not a therapeutic community," "case management," "a businesslike climate."

A REALITY OF MODERN LIFE

Above all, the practically moral (and rich) Dutch have constructed their drug policy upon the principle of "social peace." The Dutch actually hate drugs, but they also treat addiction as a reality of modern life, one that can be somewhat contained if treated primarily as a health matter.

After severe outbreaks of heroin and cocaine addiction started here with the "flower children" of the early 1970s, the Dutch came upon the idea of "harm reduction." That meant not only stressing a health response to addiction as opposed to a police response, but also giving an unusual discretion to the police. Even a heroin pusher's treatment would depend upon his behavior. In short, rewards work toward the goal of "social peace."

When I was in Holland in 1989, trying to see if there was anything applicable in the Dutch policy to the enormous American problem, there were about 6,500 hard-drug users in Amsterdam. And today? There are still about 6,500 hard-drug users. But there is a consequent reality of incalculable importance.

"In the last 15 years, for the generation under 22 years of age, the percentage using hard drugs went down from 15 percent to 2.5 percent," said Dirk H. van der Woude of the Municipal Health Service. "And the average age of hard-drug users has gone up from 26.8 years in 1981 to 34.2 years in 1993."

These figures are important because they are a reflection of the Dutch wisdom in recognizing the reality of a "time of epidemics." During such periods, the powers-that-be must try to "maintain" those already addicted, while at the same time helping the next generation to avoid addiction at all costs. It now appears that that distinction has worked.

THE WANING OF AN EPIDEMIC

How did this happen? Mr. Bruning credits anti-drug education in the schools, but he readily acknowledges other factors. "Something just happens after a while," he said, noting that throughout history epidemics at some point have begun to wane. "Then there was the fact that we separated soft and hard drugs, until we got to the point today where hard drugs are not pushed so much." (Soft drugs, like marijuana, can be bought and consumed openly, as in the coffeehouses, while hard drugs, like heroin, are not generally tolerated.)

© Rosen/Rothco. Reprinted with permission.

Then he cited the country's methadone program. The "halfway" drug to wean drug users off hard drugs such as heroin is even given out in police stations and on special buses. And, finally, he says, the very open presence of junkies on the streets of Amsterdam—a public presence that many Dutch thoroughly despise—has convinced the majority of the new generation that this is not fashionable and is not what they want to be.

The Dutch, for all their seeming liberality about and understanding of the drug culture, actually are quite wily about it. Health officials note that at the height of the drug-squatter culture here in 1983, the new mayor of Amsterdam completely nonplussed junkies by embracing the legalization of heroin.

"He wouldn't let them use him as the enemy," Mr. Bruning recalled with a wry smile. "He took away their subculture values and expectations."

There are still plenty of problems: Hard drugs are now pouring into Europe from the former Soviet Union; junkies traverse formerly closed borders, open because of the European Union; respectable Dutch people are increasingly angry about the crime spawned by the drug users with their expensive habits.

Still, what Holland could teach a more moralistic America is: Figure out what you can reasonably expect to do with the problem and the tools you have at hand, devise a program to maximize your strengths, and above all, plan so that you diminish the problem, thus sparing the next generation.

VIEWPOINT

"The Dutch have visited upon
themselves misery from drug abuse
by enacting drug laws that go
unenforced."

THE U.S. SHOULD NOT COPY
HOLLAND'S DRUG POLICIES

Lee P. Brown

Lee P. Brown was the director of drug policy for the Clinton administration from 1993 to 1996. He is a professor of sociology
at Rice University in Houston, Texas. In the following viewpoint,
Brown lists a number of myths concerning drugs and drug policy. One of these myths, he writes, is the belief that Holland and
other European countries have solved their drug problems by legalizing or decriminalizing drugs. Brown argues that Holland,
Great Britain, and Italy have actually experienced social problems as a result of liberal drug laws, and the United States
should not follow their example.

As you read, consider the following questions:
1. What problems have Holland, Great Britain, and Italy faced
   because of their drug policies, in Brown's opinion?
2. How does Brown refute the idea that drug use is a personal
   matter?
3. What issues are part of the "essential business of responsible
   policy making," according to the author?

From "Eight Myths About Drugs: There Are No Simple Solutions" by Lee P. Brown,
speech at the Drug Policy Reform Conference of the Civil Liberties Union of
Massachusetts, Cambridge, Mass., May 21, 1994.

The use of illegal drugs is a very complex policy issue. It goes to the core of our behavior as individuals, as families, as communities, and as a nation. It has global implications. Those of us who must grapple daily with the issue of illicit drug use and its consequences, and who must see it in its many dimensions, know that if we are to be effective, our responses must be thoughtful, comprehensive, balanced, and effective.

By comparison, some solutions that have been put forward to resolve the problem of drugs, and crime, and violence, seem remarkably simple. And plausible. Until they are forced into the bright light of day.

This is what I want to talk about today: simple solutions, tough problems, difficult choices.

THE MYTHOLOGY

From time to time one hears some remarkable—even bizarre—assertions by so-called drug experts about what the drug situation is. The purported solutions then follow the mythology.

Let me outline what I have come to call *Eight Myths about Drugs.* These can be put in straightforward terms.

The first myth is that everything is getting worse, and that nothing is getting better. It follows from this that the so-called drug war is a failure, and that we should abandon it in favor of another approach.

In fact, drug use data from the nation's households and secondary schools show substantial declines in overall drug use over the past decade:

• In 1979, more than 23 million Americans used some illicit drug. By 1992 the number had dropped to 11.4 million.

• Past month cocaine use, which peaked in 1985 at 8.6 million users, had dropped to 1.3 million users by 1992. This was accompanied by a similarly dramatic decline in the use of cocaine by adolescents from the mid-1980s until 1992.

• We have a severe, continuing problem with the chronic, hard-core, addicted use of drugs. We freely acknowledge this; indeed, we want this to be broadly known. The nation's estimated 2.7 million hard-core users are our most serious concern. They cause the most damage to themselves, to their families and to their communities. They are the most important single focus of our National Drug Control Strategy.

• As troubling, we have indicators of recent increases in the use of drugs by secondary school children.

• Overall, the country—not the government, not a particular Administration, but the country—has experienced major declines in non-addictive, casual use of illicit drugs. The number of users of any illicit drugs today is the same level as it was in the early 1970s.

Let us reason about this: can this really be called failure?

Now, it is sometimes alleged that one can't trust what the government data says.

In fact, the government does not collect the data. The Research Triangle Institute, an independent non-Government organization, conducts the Household Survey. The University of Michigan's Institute for Social Research conducts the survey of drug use in the nation's secondary schools.

ADDRESSING THE PROBLEMS

A second myth is that current policy—one suspects any current policy—is making things worse. This myth says that current drug policy does not address the real problems, which are violence and HIV transmission.

In fact, violence and HIV transmission are only part of the human carnage that results from drug use. Addiction, drug-exposed infants, drug-induced accidents, loss of productivity, loss of employment, family breakdown, and the degeneration of communities are others. All directly flow from drug use itself. As the number of users increases, these problems will multiply.

Current policy directly addresses these issues through specific strategies to prevent new use, to effectively treat hard-core users, and to bring overwhelming force against the street markets.

A third myth is that enforcement just adds to the problem. Drug enforcement and the application of criminal justice should be given up in favor of harm reduction approaches.

In fact, effective enforcement serves to reduce drug supply, drive up prices, reduce the number of users and decrease the effects of chronic hard-core use. There is a demonstrable inverse relationship between the price of cocaine and the number of individuals seeking emergency room treatment. The criminal justice system, moreover, provides means to remand drug offenders to effective treatment.

NO SUPPORT FOR LEGALIZATION

A fourth myth is that there is massive support for policy change by social thinkers, policy-level officials, and the public at large. This includes broad support for legalization, or the decriminalization of drug use.

In fact, there is no massive support for legalization. A 1990 Gallup poll showed that 80 percent of the public thought that legalizing drugs was a bad idea. Only 14 percent thought that it was a good idea. Among American 12th-graders surveyed in the 1992–3 school year, 84 percent said that their friends would disapprove of their smoking marijuana regularly; 94 percent said that their friends would disapprove of their taking cocaine occasionally.

Reflecting the views of the American public, there is no meaningful support within Congress for the legalization of illicit drugs.

And in fact, policy-level officials who are directly responsible for the drug issue—*beginning with the President*—oppose legalization. I do, too.

PUBLIC OPINION ABOUT DRUG LEGALIZATION

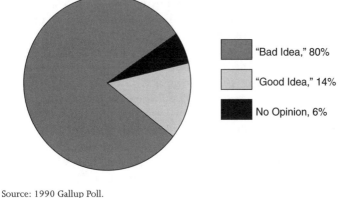

"Bad Idea," 80%

"Good Idea," 14%

No Opinion, 6%

Source: 1990 Gallup Poll.

A fifth myth is that legalizing drugs, or decriminalizing drug use, will eliminate the illegal drug markets and the violence in our streets.

I do not dispute that drug markets do, in fact, generate violence. But the way to deal with the markets and the associated violence is to dry up the pool of users through effective prevention and treatment, and through the use of street enforcement, as many communities throughout the country are now struggling to do.

A sixth myth is that legalizing drugs will be free of cost. As this myth goes, there is nothing to suggest that legalizing drugs will increase drug use, or its consequences.

In fact, the suggestion that legalizing drugs will not increase drug use is a fantastic myth.

• Our own national experience with Prohibition is indicative of what would happen if drug laws and drug enforcement were eliminated. Alcohol use data from the 1930s shows clearly that the repeal of the Volstead Act resulted in an immediate, sustained rise in the use of alcohol to levels higher than those that existed prior to Prohibition.

• We believe that the repeal of drug control laws would, likewise, result in an immediate, sustained rise in the use of drugs—and a concomitant rise in the casualties of the use of drugs.

NO GOOD MODELS

Another—seventh—myth is that there are excellent foreign models to show that decriminalization works: the Netherlands and the U.K. are two.

This is another fantastic myth. One need only read the international press to realize the degree to which the Dutch have visited upon themselves misery from drug abuse by enacting drug laws that go unenforced, and policies that encourage "responsible" use rather than discourage any use at all. The Dutch are pleased to say they have remained mostly unscathed by drug use by their own citizens. They cannot say the same of the many thousands of foreign visitors who arrive to buy drugs, steal or panhandle to keep using them, and then ask the Dutch to treat them for addiction.

And one need only recall the disastrous experience of Great Britain with the controlled distribution of heroin. In the years between 1959 and 1968—according to the 1981 British Medical Journal—the number of heroin addicts in the U.K. doubled every sixteen months. The experiment was, of course, terminated. But addiction rates in the U.K. have not subsided.

At the same time, no one mentions Italy, which permits heroin and other drugs to be used legally, and where the number of heroin addicts—some 350,000, by official estimates and the level of HIV prevalence—an estimated 70 percent—are higher than those in any other country in Western Europe. I ask myself at times why those who advocate drug policy reform are so quiet about the Italian model.

And then there is a final, eighth myth. This one says that drug use is a personal matter, and that it affects no one other than the user.

There's no good thing to say about this. Given what we know about the effects of drugs, this is simply wrong. No one familiar with alcohol abuse would suggest that alcoholism affects the user only. And no one who works with the drug-addicted would tell you that their use of drugs has not affected others—usually families and friends in the first instance. . . .

RESPONSIBLE POLICY-MAKING

Let me conclude with a few overall points.

First, *given what the overwhelming number of Americans want, and given what we have to do to address the terrible consequences of drug use, legalization is a marginal issue.* It does not get to the core of the problem. In seeking to satisfy the few, it subverts the best interests of the many. In purporting to provide a quick, simple, costless cure for crime and violence in America, it fails to suggest how *more* drug availability will not lead to *more* drug use—and more devastating consequences.

It does not deal with the essential business of responsible policy-making:

- *How* to provide effective prevention education for adolescents;
- *How* to make effective treatment available for our estimated 2.7 million hard-core drug users;
- *How* to develop effective workplace strategies that reduce accidents, reduce employer's health care costs, and improve productivity;
- *How* to ensure that health care reform provides for those in need of treatment.

And it does not deal with the essential business of bringing together health policy and criminal justice policy, to improve society as a whole.

This is the real story: the day-in-day-out, blood and guts of policy-making that deals directly with the very complex issues of human behavior, that recognizes that there are no simple solutions.

In 1917, the renowned American journalist and social observer, H.L. Mencken, remarked, "There is always an easy solution to every human problem—neat, plausible, and wrong."

To the overwhelming number of Americans, to the Clinton Administration, to the American Congress, to American policy makers of this as well as prior Administrations, to Americans involved with drug programs across the country, to Americans in drug-blighted communities across the country, legalization is exactly such a solution—neat, plausible, and wrong. . . .

What we need to do is to get on with the business of reducing drug availability, preventing drug use, treating addicts, of restoring the value of the American family—in short, of addressing some of the most basic and pressing issues of the country.

PERIODICAL BIBLIOGRAPHY

The following articles have been selected to supplement the diverse views presented in this chapter. Addresses are provided for periodicals not indexed in the *Readers' Guide to Periodical Literature*, the *Alternative Press Index*, the *Social Sciences Index*, or the *Index to Legal Periodicals and Books*.

Dan Baum	"The War on Drugs," *ABA Journal*, March 1993. Available from 750 N. Lake Shore Dr., Chicago, IL 60611.
Alan Cowell	"Zurich's Open Drug Policy Goes into Withdrawal," *New York Times*, March 12, 1995.
Steve Diamond	"Taking the High Road," *New Age Journal*, March/April 1996.
Joseph D. Douglass Jr.	"How Goes the 'War on Drugs'?" *Conservative Review*, January 1992. Available from 1307 Dolley Madison Blvd., Rm. 203, McLean, VA 22101.
Economist	"The Wages of Prohibition," December 24, 1994–January 6, 1995.
Tim W. Ferguson	"Caught in the Eddy of a Drug War," *Wall Street Journal*, September 6, 1994.
Stephen Flynn	"Worldwide Drug Scourge: The Response," *Brookings Review*, Spring 1993.
Tim Golden	"Mexican Connection Grows as Cocaine Supplier to U.S.," *New York Times*, July 30, 1995.
Tim Golden	"To Help Keep Mexico Stable, U.S. Soft-Pedaled Drug War," *New York Times*, July 31, 1995.
Haven Bradford Gow	"Drug Experiment in Switzerland: A Glaring Failure," *Conservative Review*, January 1992.
Paul B. Stares	"Drug Legalization: Time for a Real Debate," *Brookings Review*, Spring 1996.
Jacob Sullum	"Voodoo Social Policy," *Reason*, October 1994.
Mike Tidwell	"Our Tax Dollars Have Promoted Drug Use and Violence," *Washington Spectator*, September 1, 1994. Available from PO Box 20065, New York, NY 10011.

FOR FURTHER DISCUSSION

CHAPTER 1

1. What risks does John Leland say are associated with heroin use? In what ways have the risks of heroin use been exaggerated, according to Stanton Peele? Did reading these two viewpoints change your opinion regarding the dangers of heroin? Explain your answer.

2. Anna Quindlen describes the problem of alcohol abuse among college students. Dwight Heath presents the health benefits of moderate alcohol consumption. Do these authors fundamentally agree or disagree with each other concerning the potential dangers of alcohol? Explain your answer.

3. Some people favor legalizing marijuana because they believe it has medicinal qualities that can decrease pain and nausea. Do you think the potential benefits of marijuana outweigh its potential risks? Explain your reasoning.

CHAPTER 2

1. Most experts identify alcoholism as a disease. How do you think the "disease" label affects people struggling with alcoholism?

2. The authors in this chapter provide a wide variety of possible explanations for why some people become addicted to drugs and/or alcohol. Which of the viewpoints do you find most persuasive? Why? Do you believe that there is one cause for addiction or several contributing causes? Explain your responses.

3. The *Mindszenty Report* contends that the media share much of the blame for alcohol and drug abuse among teenagers. Consider the media that you are exposed to: television programs, music videos and recordings, movies, books, and magazines. Are you exposed to advertisements, lyrics, and other messages that promote the use or abuse of drugs or alcohol? How do you think these messages affect you, if at all?

CHAPTER 3

1. A general comment that is sometimes made about chemically addicted people is that they just need "willpower" or need to "pull themselves up by their bootstraps." Explain what these sayings mean. Do you think the concept of "willpower" is important when considering possible treatment options for alcoholics or drug addicts? Why or why not?

2. Alcoholics Anonymous (AA) has long been the most widely

accepted treatment for alcoholics in the United States. AA advocates abstinence from alcohol, as does the viewpoint by Beth Baker. Compare Baker's views to those of Audrey Kishline. Based on these viewpoints, do you think alcoholics can learn to drink moderately, or must they abstain? Explain your answer.

CHAPTER 4

1. Those who oppose legalizing drugs fear that legalization will cause a huge increase in the number of addicts. How do proponents of legalization refute this argument? Compare the viewpoints of William London and Donna E. Shalala. Which viewpoint is more persuasive? Did it significantly change your opinion concerning legalization? Explain your response.

2. The article from the *Revolutionary Worker* cites statistics to show that America's drug laws are unjust and aimed at punishing minority drug users. Cristopher Rapp also uses statistics to explain his view that drug laws are not racist. Did either author's use of statistics sway your opinion? Which author uses statistics to a greater advantage?

3. Ernesto Samper is the president of Colombia. How does his position affect your opinion of his viewpoint? Does his position make his views more or less credible than those of John P. Sweeney, who is a policy analyst at a think tank? Why or why not?

ORGANIZATIONS TO CONTACT

The editors have compiled the following list of organizations concerned with the issues debated in this book. The descriptions are derived from materials provided by the organizations. All have publications or information available for interested readers. The list was compiled on the date of publication of the present volume; names, addresses, phone and fax numbers, and e-mail and internet addresses may change. Be aware that many organizations take several weeks or longer to respond to inquiries, so allow as much time as possible.

Alcoholics Anonymous (AA)
General Service Office, PO Box 459, Grand Central Station, New York, NY 10163
(212) 870-3400 • fax: (212) 870-3003

Alcoholics Anonymous is an international fellowship of people who are recovering from alcoholism. Because AA's primary goal is to help alcoholics, it does not sponsor research or engage in education about alcoholism. AA does, however, publish books, pamphlets, and a catalog of literature concerning the organization.

American Civil Liberties Union (ACLU)
132 W. 43rd St., New York, NY 10036
(212) 944-9800 • fax: (212) 869-9065

The ACLU, one of the oldest civil liberties organizations in the United States, favors decriminalizing drugs. It believes that efforts to wage a "war on drugs" have increased the government's power to intrude in Americans' private lives and that this intrusiveness is eroding people's civil rights. The ACLU publishes information packets on drug legalization and decriminalization.

American Council for Drug Education
136 E. 64th St., New York, NY 10021
(800) 488-3784 • (212) 758-8060 • fax: (212) 758-6784

The American Council for Drug Education focuses on educating the public about the harmfulness of abusing drugs and alcohol. It publishes educational materials, reviews scientific findings, and develops educational media campaigns. The council's pamphlets, monographs, films, and other teaching aids address educators, parents, physicians, and employees.

American Council on Alcohol Problems (ACAP)
3426 Bridgeland Dr., Bridgeton, MO 63044
(314) 739-5944 • fax: (314) 739-0848

ACAP is the successor to temperance organizations such as the American Temperance League and the Anti-Saloon League. It is composed of state temperance organizations, religious bodies, and fraternal organizations that support ACAP's philosophy of abstinence from alcohol.

ACAP works to restrict the availability of alcohol in the United States by controlling alcohol advertising and educating the public concerning the harmfulness of alcohol abuse. ACAP serves as a clearinghouse for information and research materials. It publishes the monthlies *ACAP Recap* and the *American Issue*.

Center on Addiction and Substance Abuse (CASA)
Columbia University, 152 W. 57th St., New York, NY 10019
(212) 841-5200 • fax: (212) 956-8020
CASA is a private, nonprofit organization that works to educate the public about the hazards of chemical dependency. The organization supports treatment as the best way to reduce chemical dependency in America. CASA conducts research into chemical dependency and produces many publications on the harmfulness of alcohol and drug addiction and effective ways to address the problem.

Drug Enforcement Administration (DEA)
1405 I St. NW, Washington, DC 20537
(202) 633-1000
The DEA is the federal agency charged with enforcing the nation's drug laws. It concentrates its efforts on restricting the flow of illegal drugs into the United States and on curbing their distribution. It publishes *Drug Enforcement Magazine* three times a year.

Drug Policy Foundation
4801 Massachusetts Ave. NW, #400, Washington, DC 20016
(202) 895-1634
The foundation supports legalizing many illegal drugs and increasing the number of treatment programs for addicts. It distributes material on legislation regarding drug legalization. The foundation's publications include the bimonthly *Drug Policy Letter* and the book *The Great Drug War*. It also distributes *Press Clips*, an annual compilation of newspaper articles on drug legalization issues.

Hazelden Educational Materials
PO Box 176, Center City, MN 55012
(800) 328-9000 • (612) 257-4010
Hazelden is a treatment center for alcoholism and drug addiction. Hazelden Educational Materials publishes and distributes a broad variety of materials on chemical dependency and recovery. A free catalog of these materials can be obtained by calling the toll-free number.

International Narcotics Enforcement Officers Association (INEOA)
112 State St., Suite 1200, Albany, NY 12207
(518) 463-6232
INEOA examines national and international narcotics laws and seeks ways to improve those laws and to prevent drug abuse. It also studies law enforcement methods to find the most effective ways to reduce illegal drug use. The association publishes a newsletter and the monthlies *International Drug Report* and *NarcOfficer*.

Narcotics Anonymous (NA)
PO Box 9999, Van Nuys, CA 91409
(818) 780-3951

NA, comprising more than eighteen thousand groups worldwide, is an organization of recovering drug addicts who meet regularly to help each other abstain from all drugs. It publishes the monthlies *NA Way Magazine* and *Newsline*.

National Acupuncture Detoxification Association (NADA)
PO Box 1927, Vancouver, WA 98668-1927
(206) 254-0186

NADA promotes acupuncture as a treatment for drug abuse. It favors government-funded drug treatment programs and opposes drug legalization. NADA publishes the annual *NADA Newsletter*.

National Clearinghouse for Alcohol and Drug Information (NCADI)
PO Box 2345, Rockville, MD 20847-2345
(800) 729-6686 • fax: (301) 468-3059

NCADI is an information service of the Office for Substance Abuse Prevention of the U.S. Department of Health and Human Services. The clearinghouse provides alcohol and drug prevention materials as well as educational materials free, including technical reports, pamphlets, and posters. It publishes a bimonthly newsletter, *Prevention Pipeline: An Alcohol and Drug Awareness Service*, containing the latest available research, resources, and activities in the prevention field.

National Council on Alcoholism and Drug Dependence (NCADD)
12 W. 21st St., 7th Fl., New York, NY 10010
(800) 622-2255 • (212) 206-6770 • fax: (212) 645-1690

The National Council on Alcoholism and Drug Dependence is a nonprofit organization whose goal is to educate Americans about alcohol and drug abuse. It provides community-based prevention and education programs as well as information and service referrals. NCADD publishes pamphlets, fact sheets, and other materials that provide statistics and facts on chemical dependency.

National Organization for the Reform of Marijuana Laws (NORML)
2001 S St. NW, Suite 640, Washington, DC 20009
(202) 483-5500

NORML fights to legalize marijuana and to help those who have been convicted and sentenced for possessing or selling marijuana. In addition to pamphlets and position papers, it publishes a newsletter, *Marijuana Highpoints*, and a quarterly, *NORML's Active Resistance*.

Office for Substance Abuse Prevention (OSAP)
PO Box 2345, Rockville, MD 20847-2345
(800) 729-6686 • (301) 468-2600
TDD: (800) 487-4889 or (301) 230-2867

OSAP leads the U.S. government's efforts to prevent chemical dependency among Americans. To this end, it provides the public with information on chemical dependency, including its publication of scientific findings, databases, the bimonthly *Prevention Pipeline*, videotapes, fact sheets, brochures, monographs, pamphlets, and posters.

Office of National Drug Control Policy
Executive Office of the President, Washington, DC 20500
(202) 467-9800
The Office of National Drug Control Policy is responsible for the government's national drug strategy. Headed by the drug "czar," the office formulates the president's antidrug policy and coordinates the federal agencies responsible for stopping drug trafficking. Drug policy studies are available upon request.

RAND Corporation
Distribution Services, 1700 Main St., Santa Monica, CA 90406-2138
(310) 393-0411, ext. 6686
The RAND Corporation is a nonprofit research institution that seeks to improve public policy through research and analysis. RAND's Drug Policy Research Center (DPRC) publishes material on the costs, prevention, and treatment of alcohol and drug abuse as well as on trends in drug-law enforcement. Its extensive list of publications includes the book *Sealing the Borders* by Peter Reuter.

Rutgers Center of Alcoholic Studies
Smithers Hall, Busch Campus, Piscataway, NJ 08854
(201) 932-2190
The center is an international source of information on alcohol studies. Its international research focuses on the causes and treatment of alcoholism, the effects of alcohol consumption on the human body, and ways to prevent alcohol abuse. The center offers courses on the study and treatment of alcoholism and provides information to the public through its library and its publications, which include books, monographs, pamphlets, and the bimonthly *Journal of Studies on Alcohol*.

Secular Organization for Sobriety (SOS)
PO Box 5, Buffalo, NY 14215
(716) 834-2922
SOS is a nonprofit network of groups dedicated to helping individuals achieve and maintain sobriety. The organization believes that alcoholics can best recover by rationally choosing to make sobriety rather than alcohol a priority. Most members of SOS reject the religious basis of Alcoholics Anonymous and other similar self-help groups. SOS publishes the quarterly *SOS National Newsletter* and distributes the books *Unhooked: Staying Sober and Drug Free* and SOS founder James Christopher's *How to Stay Sober: Recovery Without Religion*.

BIBLIOGRAPHY OF BOOKS

Dan Baum   *Smoke and Mirrors: The War on Drugs and the Politics of Failure.* Boston: Little, Brown, 1996.

Ronald Bayer and Gerald M. Oppenheimer, eds.   *Confronting Drug Policy: Illicit Drugs in a Free Society.* New York: Cambridge University Press, 1993.

Henri Begleiter and Benjamin Kissin   *The Genetics of Alcoholism.* New York: Oxford University Press, 1995.

Daniel K. Benjamin and Roger LeRoy Miller   *Undoing Drugs: Beyond Legalization.* New York: Basic-Books, 1991.

Eva Bertram et al.   *Drug War Politics: The Price of Denial.* Berkeley and Los Angeles: University of California Press, 1996.

Kenneth Blum   *Alcohol and the Addictive Brain: New Hope for Alcoholics from Biogenetic Research.* New York: Free Press, 1991.

David Boaz, ed.   *The Crisis in Drug Prohibition.* Washington, DC: Cato Institute, 1990.

Tony Bouza   *A Carpet of Blue: An Ex-Cop Takes a Tough Look at America's Drug Problem.* Minneapolis: Deaconess Press, 1992.

Don Calahan   *An Ounce of Prevention: Strategies for Solving Tobacco, Alcohol, and Drug Problems.* San Francisco: Jossey-Bass, 1991.

James Christopher   *SOS Sobriety: The Proven Alternative to 12-Step Programs.* Buffalo, NY: Prometheus Books, 1992.

Peter R. Cohen   *Helping Your Chemically Dependent Teenager Recover: A Guide for Parents and Other Concerned Adults.* Minneapolis: Johnson Institute, 1991.

John. C. Crabbe Jr. and R. Adron Harris, eds.   *The Genetic Basis of Alcohol and Drug Addictions.* New York: Plenum, 1991.

Elliott Currie   *Reckoning: Drugs, the Cities, and the American Future.* New York: Hill & Wang, 1993.

Norman K. Denzin   *The Alcoholic Society: Addiction and Recovery of the Self.* New Brunswick, NJ: Transaction Publishers, 1993.

Jerry Dorsman   *How to Quit Drinking Without AA: A Complete Self-Help Guide.* Newark, DE: New Dawn, 1993.

Scott Dowling, ed.   *The Psychology and Treatment of Addictive Behavior.* Madison, CT: International Universities Press, 1995.

Steven B. Duke and Albert C. Gross, eds.   *America's Longest War: Rethinking Our Tragic Crusade Against Drugs.* New York: Jeremy P. Tarcher/Putnam Books, 1993.

Griffith Edwards and Malcolm H. Lader, eds.	*Addiction: Processes of Change.* New York: Oxford University Press, 1994.
Jeffrey M. Elliot	*Drugs and American Society.* Boston: Allyn & Bacon, 1994.
Mathea Falco	*The Making of a Drug-Free America: Programs That Work.* New York: Random House, 1992.
John C. Flynn	*Cocaine: An In-Depth Look at the Facts, Science, History, and Future of the World's Most Addictive Drug.* New York: Carol Publishing, 1991.
Dean R. Gerstein and Lawrence W. Green, eds.	*Preventing Drug Abuse.* Washington, DC: National Academy Press, 1993.
Diana R. Gordon	*The Dangerous Classes: Drug Prohibition and Policy Politics.* New York: Norton, 1994.
Jessica de Grazia	*DEA: The War Against Drugs.* London: BBC Books, 1991.
Daniel P. Greenfield, ed.	*Prescription Drug Abuse and Dependence: How Prescription Drug Abuse Contributes to the Drug Abuse Epidemic.* Springfield, IL: Charles C. Thomas, 1995.
Lester Grinspoon and James B. Bakalar	*Marihuana: The Forbidden Medicine.* New Haven, CT: Yale University Press, 1993.
James A. Inciardi, Dorothy Lockwood, and Anne E. Pottienger	*Women and Crack Cocaine.* New York: Prentice Hall, 1992.
Jerry Johnston	*It's Killing Our Kids.* Irving, TX: Word Publishing, 1991.
Lloyd D. Johnston	*National Survey Results on Drug Use from Monitoring the Future Study, 1975–1994.* Rockville, MD: National Institute on Drug Abuse, 1995.
Mark A.R. Kleiman	*Against Excess: Drug Policy for Results.* New York: Basic-Books, 1992.
David Krogh	*Smoking: The Artificial Passion.* New York: W.H. Freeman, 1991.
Clarence Lusane with Dennis Desmond	*Pipe Dream Blues: Racism and the War on Drugs.* Boston: South End Press, 1991.
George McGovern	*Terry: My Daughter's Life-and-Death Struggle with Alcoholism.* New York: Villard, 1996.
Kenneth J. Meier	*The Politics of Sin: Drugs, Alcohol, and Public Policy.* Armonk, NY: M.E. Sharpe, 1994.
Richard Lawrence Miller	*The Case for Legalizing Drugs.* New York: Praeger, 1991.

Richard Lawrence Miller — *Drug Warriors and Their Prey: From Police Power to Police State.* New York: Praeger, 1996.

Office of National Drug Control Policy — *Consult with America: A Look at How Americans View the Country's Drug Problem.* Washington, DC: National Criminal Justice Reference Service, 1996.

Office of National Drug Control Policy — *Reducing the Impact of Drugs on American Society.* Washington, DC: National Criminal Justice Reference Service, 1995.

Stanton Peele — *Diseasing of America: Addiction Treatment Out of Control.* Lexington, MA: Lexington Books, 1989.

Stanton Peele and Archie Brodsky, with Mary Arnold — *The Truth About Addiction and Recovery: The Life Process Program for Outgrowing Destructive Habits.* New York: Simon & Schuster, 1992.

Raphael F. Perl, ed. — *Drugs and Foreign Policy: A Critical Review.* Boulder, CO: Westview Press, 1994.

Marc A. Schuckit — *Educating Yourself About Alcohol and Drugs: A People's Primer.* New York: Plenum, 1995.

Sam Staley — *Drug Policy and the Decline of American Cities.* New Brunswick, NJ: Transaction Publishers, 1992.

Paul B. Stares — *Global Habit: The Drug Problem in a Borderless World.* Washington, DC: Brookings Institution, 1996.

Robert M. Stutman and Richard Esposito — *Dead on Delivery: Inside the Drug Wars, Straight from the Street.* New York: Warner Books, 1992.

Harold H. Traver and Mark S. Gaylord, eds. — *Drugs, Law, and the State.* New Brunswick, NJ: Transaction Publishers, 1992.

Arnold S. Trebach and James A. Inciardi — *Legalize It? Debating American Drug Policy.* Washington, DC: American University Press, 1993.

Jack Trimpey — *The Small Book: A Revolutionary Alternative for Overcoming Alcohol and Drug Dependence.* Rev. ed. New York: Dell, 1996.

Dan Waldorf, Craig Reinarman, and Sheigla Murphy — *Cocaine Changes: The Experience of Using and Quitting.* Philadelphia: Temple University Press, 1991.

Bob Wright and Deborah George Wright — *Dare to Confront: How to Intervene When Someone You Care About Has an Alcohol or Drug Problem.* New York: MasterMedia, 1990.

Franklin E. Zimring and Gordon Hawkins — *The Search for Rational Drug Control.* New York: Cambridge University Press, 1992.

INDEX

addiction, 56-57, 58
  common characteristics of, 59-60
  and withdrawal/relapse cycle, 60-61
  cost to society of, 84
  as disease, 50-53, 57, 85
  crosses societal boundaries, 51, 87
  effects of, 52-53
  natural basis of, 55-56, 62, 130
  and sex/love, 59
  and overdosing, 23, 24, 25, 26, 137
    see also Cobain, Kurt
  roots of, 51-52
  treatments for, 53, 106-11
    acupuncture, 83-89
      detoxification procedure, 88
      as low-cost alternative, 84, 89
      as part of comprehensive
        program, 86
      long-term nature of, 87
    religion, 96-99
    see also alcohol abuse; biofeedback;
      drugs; twelve-step programs
Addictive Behaviors Research Center,
  55
adolescents. See teenagers
African Americans, 147, 152, 155
  and high percentage of crack
    prosecutions, 153
  systemic racism against, 148, 149
AIDS/HIV, 41, 43, 86, 87, 104
  from injection-drug use, 17, 19, 20,
    139, 174
  and legalization of heroin, 176
alcohol, 20, 24, 64-66, 138
  abuse, 51, 52, 53, 61, 137
    and cultural factors, 63-66
    as disease, 57-58, 119, 126
    as hidden problem, 113-14
    as serious problem, 27-29
    signs of, 116
    social effects of, 176
    treatments for, 94, 95, 107-108
      intervention by family/friends,
        53, 112-16
      Moderation Management (MM),
        123-30
        growth of, 129
        for problem (not chronic)
          drinkers, 124, 125
        provides supportive
          environment, 127-28
      see also addiction; teenagers; twelve-
        step programs
  benefits of, 30-32, 129-30

  media's glamorization of, 75
  Alcohol Health & Research World, 126
  Alcoholics Anonymous. *See* twelve-step
    programs
  American Council on Science and
    Health (ACSH), 30, 134, 136
  American Medical Association, 43
    journal of (*JAMA*), 103
  American Museum of Natural History,
    59
  American Psychological Association,
    110
  Ancona, Gregory, 25, 26
  Andean Trade Preferences Act (ATPA),
    160, 163
  Andrews, Colman, 32
  Anslinger, Harry, 136
  Association for Applied
    Psychophysiology and Biofeedback
    (AAPB), 92
  attention deficit disorder (ADD), 91
  aversion therapy, 111

  Baca, Catherine, 110
  Bakalar, James B., 39
  Baker, Beth, 117
  Bartholomew, Anita, 93
  Benjamin, Daniel K., 52
  biofeedback, 90-95
    reprograms brain, 93-94
    various applications of, 92
  Block, Sherman, 156
  Bloom, Floyd E., 61
  Bowman Gray School of Medicine
    (North Carolina), 56, 108
  Bradley, Katharine A., 126
  brain, 55, 93-94, 97, 110
  Brecher, Edward M., 24, 25-26
  Brody, Jane E., 112
  Brown, Lee P., 172
  Bruning, Ernst, 169, 170, 171
  Bureau of Narcotics, 136
  Bush, George, 73

  California, 61, 152, 153, 157
    see also Los Angeles
  Carleton University (Ottawa, Canada),
    142
  Cataldo, Michael F., 58, 60
  CBS, 77
  Center on Addiction and Substance
    Abuse (CASA), 19, 28, 44, 45
  Center on Alcohol Abuse, Chemical
    Dependency, and Addiction
    (University of New Mexico), 57, 97,

increase in, 18
  began in 1970s, 169
  among crack addicts, 19
  due to increased purity/low price,
    17
  social effects of, 101
  risks of, 20
  as serious problem, 17-21
  see also methadone treatment
Hirsch, Charles, 24
Hispanic Americans, 147, 152
Hitzig, Pietr, 110
Holland, 45-46
  drug policies of
  U.S. should copy, 168-71
  con, 172-77
homelessness, 156-57
Howland, Jane, 18

ibogaine (African hallucinogen), 109
Inciardi, James A., 36
Institute of Medicine (IOM), 102
  Committee on the Federal Regulation
    of Methadone Treatment, 100
Investigational New Drug (IND), 41
Italy, 176

Jackson, Janet, 76
Jackson, Michael, 76
Japan, 98
Jefferson Medical Center
  (Philadelphia), 25
Johns Hopkins Medical Institutions,
  54, 106, 109, 110
Johnson, Kelly, 69, 70
Johnston, Lloyd, 18
Journal of Abnormal Psychology, 65

Kamiya, Joe, 94
Kansas City, Missouri, 95
Kilbourne, Jean, 75
Kleber, Herbert, 19, 20
Kleiman, Mark A.R., 19
Kricfalusi, John, 77
Kishline Audrey, 123

LAMM (longer-acting analog of
  methadone), 102
Langenbahn, Stacia, 29
Lansdowne, Virginia, 97
Larson, David, 99
Latin America, 139, 159, 162
Leland, John, 17
Lemonheads, The (rock group), 73
Liang, Bryan A., 155, 157
Licit and Illicit Drugs (Brecher), 24
Life Sciences Institute of Mind-Body
  Health, 95

Lincoln Hospital (New York), 84
London, William, 134
Los Angeles, 35, 36, 154, 156
  Las Familias del Pueblo family service
    agency, 157
  Santa Monica High School, 34
Los Angeles Times, 152, 153, 155
Los Angeles Times Magazine, 32
Lubar, Joel, 92

Manella, Nora M., 153
Manhattan Institute's City Journal, 78
Mantle, Mickey, 64
Marihuana, the Forbidden Medicine
  (Grinspoon and Bakalar), 39
marijuana, 39, 169
  campaign against, 44
    misguided nature of, 45, 46
  effects of, 42, 137
    are beneficial, 40, 41, 43
    are harmful, 33-38, 142-43, 144
  historical background of, 40
  see also addiction; teenagers
Marijuana Tax Act, 136
Marinol (cannabis-based drug), 42
Marlatt, G. Alan, 55, 65
Martin, Billy, 142
Maryland, 120, 121, 122
Matthews, Roy, 97
Mayo Clinic, 92
McBride, Duane C., 36
McCaffrey, Barry, 18, 20
media
  glamorization of drugs in, 72-79
    through music, 73-76
    through TV, 76-78
    see also New York Times
Media & Values, 75
Media Virus: Hidden Agendas in the Popular
  Culture (Rushkoff), 76, 77
Mencken, H.L., 177
Mental Health Services Administration,
  101
methadone treatment, 100-105, 170-
  71
  two basic types of, 103
Mexico, 139, 160, 162, 167
Miami, Florida, 85
Miller, Roger Leroy, 52
Miller, William R., 58, 107, 108, 110
  on moderate drinking for alcoholics,
    57
  on role of spirituality in recovery, 97,
    99
Mindszenty, Joseph Cardinal, 79
Mindszenty Report, 72
Mississippi Medical Center, 119
Mitchell, Ellinor R., 82